River Pigs and Cayuses

RIVER PIGS and CAYU-SES

ORAL HISTORIES FROM THE PACIFIC NORTHWEST

RON STRICKLAND

Photographs by the author

LEXIKOS
San Francisco

First published in 1984 by
Lexikos
1012 14th Street
San Francisco, CA 94114

Edited by Tom Hassett
Designed by CABA
Production by Carlton Herrick/QR Inc.
Text set in Bembo by Elan Graphic
Resources
Printed and bound by Edwards Bros.

Library of Congress Cataloging in Publication Data
Main entry under title:

River pigs and cayuses.

     1. Northwest, Pacific—Social life and customs.
2. Northwest, Pacific—Biography. 3. Pioneers—Northwest, Pacific—Biography.
4. Oral history. I. Strickland, Ron.
F852.R62   1984   979.5'041'0922   84-48239
ISBN 0-938530-29-1

84 85 86 87 5 4 3 2 1

To the young and old storytellers
whose tales are yet to be told

Contents

Ron Strickland

Introduction

We are all storytellers if given half a chance. All we need is a listener.

Listening is not as easy as it looks. It takes infinite patience. Most of all the listener must care. It is an art of subtle encouragement. In a roomful of people the happiest person is to be found beside a good listener.

I must be a good listener because all kinds of people, total strangers, are always telling me about themselves. A few years ago I became so fascinated with these stories that I decided to begin recording them. I was not after a precise, orderly record of the past nor was I attuned to common subjects of conversation such as pets, genealogy, kids, or gossip. I did want to find good, pithy stories, steeped in the individualism of someone's own ferment of ideas, associations, and years.

Originally storytellers came my way purely by accident in places like Polebridge, Bonners Ferry, Metaline Falls, Republic, Nighthawk, Twisp, Concrete, Sedro Woolley, La Conner, Seattle, and Friday Harbor in Montana, Idaho, and Washington. Between 1970 and 1983 I spent as much time as possible exploring and choosing routes for a new long-distance pathway, the Pacific Northwest Trail. But soon my fascination

1

with the region grew into a quest to preserve part of the oral traditions I had loved so much as a footloose rambler. Having emigrated from the overdeveloped East, I feared the drastic effects of new roads, summer homes, strip mines, forest rape, water pollution, and other imminent threats. I feared that a time would soon come when so much tradition would be lost that there would be plenty of old people but very few old-timers.

That happened much sooner than I expected. Many of the friends whose stories grace this book have already gone. I was very close to some of them; they filled important gaps in my own life. But please don't ask who survives and who doesn't. Think of them *all* as lively, optimistic souls whom you are meeting here in person.

Each time someone dies an irreplaceable world disappears. The stories in this book are offered as inspiration to people everywhere to sit down immediately and start listening. And recording, if possible. Do it even if you don't think you need the stories or information, even if you think there will always be plenty of time for this later.

In 1979 I visited Chief Charlie Jones of the Pacheenaht Band at Port Renfrew on the West Coast of Vancouver Island. If that alert, busy man had not told me, I would never have guessed that he was over one hundred years old. In fact, I found him energetically carving a piece of wood in his workshop. As an active revivalist for Coast Salish traditions, he wanted the government to build a center where he could teach young people traditional fishing methods. He showed me a dozen fir knots he had found in the forest and stored in a box. ''We used to use these for halibut hooks,'' he said. ''They are extremely hard and won't rot.'' He teased the dense brown wood with his knife to prove how much tougher it was than ordinary fir. ''Whenever I go through the forest and see one of these knots I pick it up to use later.''

The stories we record now are like those knots. When our relatives, friends, and neighbors are gone (or when we, too, are no more) the knots will endure and be valued.

Sometimes at the height of my search for storytellers in 1978 and 1979 I time-travelled in and out of several different lives in the course

2

of a single day. Imagine the heady intensity of dizzying blurs of months spent haunting woodlots, back porches, corrals, fishing schooners, ranch kitchens, Scout camps, log cabins, saltwater beaches, overgrown Indian trails, game refuges, forgotten mines, and wilderness mountains. Even when I was very ill I kept at it, as on that chilly autumn day when I straggled, virus-weary, down out of the snowbound Pasayten Wilderness in search of refuge. But immediately I was on the trail of the Methow Valley's old-time cowboys. The scruffy, dusty little town of Twisp looked like the set for a 1950's Jimmy Dean movie; it was the right place. I soon felt like an 1880's placer miner with a sluice box full of "colors." I'd found Bill Robler, the dean of rodeo bullhorn callers, Deke Smith, the ace storyteller whose slow, gravelly voice is a national treasure, and Ross Filer, the Methow Valley Zane Grey.

But story mining is as full of disappointments as prospecting. The worst words to hear are, "Oh, you should have been here last month before old so-and-so died; now *he* could have told you some stories." Almost as bad is finding someone whose stories have disappeared in the fogs of a stormy mind.

Not a few old-timers helped me despite very serious physical weaknesses. One islander who had spent most of his life on or beside the saltchuck was alone with a picture-only TV when I found him in a nursing home. The sound was off because he was almost stone deaf, and he was alone not because of that or his partial paralysis but because of the disinterest of anyone in visiting him. Yet he was a good-natured fellow and very eager to help me. Though the four walls of his room were only a few miles away from the best scenes of his youth, he had no way to travel. When I checked him out of the nursing home for an outing many envious people watched us go. Later it was almost more than I could manage to carry him to a log overlooking a great bay where cormorants ("skags") shot across the surface of the water and fishing boats crawled across the island-studded horizon.

I could smell the acrid odor of incontinence. The heavy, helpless man's deafness was almost as total as my hoarseness. But the great waves crashed on the beach and the sun shone bravely just as they always had at this spot. Then the memories came and the infirmities dropped away like the spray flung from a cresting wave. The beach itself changed with the boats and the fish traps and the men who had worked here. Slowly the bonds of time cracked open like oysters, the pearls inside made of words.

I would like to think that some readers will read these stories aloud to capture the cadences and effects of the original experience I heard. Passing that opportunity on to you is a major purpose of this book. Another purpose is good, enjoyable entertainment. And then there are the Big Themes. I do not want to frighten anyone with them, but I hope you will be fascinated, as I have been, by a few common threads which run throughout the book.

For the last several years our national news has often been a litany of economic woes, international reverses, environmental degradation, official corruption, social unrest, and personal insecurity. Against all of these conundrums this book offers nothing more substantial than cowhand Ross Filer pouring cow camp coffee out of a blackened pot while the "hoot hooters" drum in the distance. Or Gaspar Petta of Jasper's Pass explaining how his balloon silk underwear and lynx-fur face mask kept him warm on North Cascades traplines. Or Eva Beebee telling why a neighbor celebrated the Beebees' wedding on the North Fork of the Flathead with dynamite.

I believe that solutions to our national problems must begin with similar will power, optimism, maturity, gumption, and sense of humor. Although these traditional values are "square" and unglamorous, my guess is that America yearns for them with both nostalgia and anticipation. We have sources of strength which must be heard from our neighbors' lips to be understood and appreciated.

Many people in this book show a gentleness which comes from a lifetime of trials. An inner grace shines forth in their accounts. Listen for it as Gaspar Petta rides out an avalanche in the North Cascades. Or when professional gambler Mark Gilkey decides to fold up his "hot town" poker games for the last time. Or when Al Coffelt struggles to get by in the moneyless San Juan Islands on "popcorn and ice." Or when Gene Grush celebrates the equality and helpfulness of the railroad hoboes in their trackside "jungles." I find these qualities, too, in the younger people, like the Mores, whose contemporary solutions to old problems I have included here.

Failed crops, cruel layoffs, shattered dreams, and broken lives are the dark side of America's traditional promise of abundance for all, and all too often even simple survival is a major victory. As sheepman Tom Drumheller says, "People who went through the depression of the thirties all have a kind of kindred spirit. We learned then what being frugal amounts to." Deke Smith remembers, "Everybody. . . was poor as the devil." Rancher Slim Worthen says, "We didn't use much equipment, and there was little expense so we didn't have to have a great big income. We took it out of our hides, though, working out — she teaching school and me working in the woods."

Cooperative effort is a related theme of many of these stories. Putting up a barn in a moneyless wilderness or forming a volunteer fire department or holding a bake sale are only possible if neighbors work together. But there is a deeper current here, too. Listen carefully to Clara Fewkes and the others for the caring which elevates their sharing above mere practicality.

Voluntary associations are quintessentially American. Even our government reflects this, being a voluntary association of free citizens through a constitutional convention. Ever since the Mayflower Compact the exigencies of distance, wilderness, and necessity have encouraged the development of voluntarism in America. (It is unfortunate, however, that the lawsuit is now coming to be more symbolic of our society than the barn-raising.)

Eighty-five year old ex-wrangler Bill Robler laments that "in the old days everybody trusted everybody because there was no need for mistrust." His friend Deke Smith remembers neighbors getting together for winter house parties. "People thought nothing of going out at ten below zero, maybe in a snowstorm, eight or ten miles through the snow to some house. The whole tribe'd go and wedge in there, Grandpa, Grandma, babies, and the whole works." Ralph Thayer recalls how his neighbors helped to raise his house and vice versa. "We didn't exchange any money. We didn't have any. They helped me and I helped them." Wilderness wife Eva Beebee says, "Nobody locked their cabins in case people needed to get in. They always left some wood split and some food for anybody who came along." Old-timer Clara Fewkes explains that "that kind of neighborliness began to decline when things prospered more. . . and when people moved away and newcomers came in who didn't understand the ways of the West."

Memory, experience, and the narrative urge are the raw materials which novelists, poets, entertainers, and balladeers carve and burnish into rich gems of invention. I believe that at its best nothing can surpass the warmth and drama of a single voice speaking directly to us of the things which matter. The campfire flickers on the rapt faces. The radio reader charms and gladdens through the limpid pulses of the air. A pastor delivers a sermon full of passion and life. A parent invents a fable for the falling-asleep child. Our impersonal age cries out for this balm, the healing touch of words, the storyteller's art.

Ron Strickland

Seattle, Washington
July 1984

Bert Jones

Fish Pirate

Many veterans of hard times have taken an illegal turn or two along the path of survival. For some it was a matter of sheer life or death. For a few such as 94-year-old Bert Jones of Anacortes, Washington, the sheer enjoyment of outwitting the system was part of the reward.

Bert Jones began his working life as a cannery hand on the coast of northwestern Washington at a time when an inconceivable wealth of salmon literally clogged bays and rivers. The bounty seemed endless but it only lasted a few decades once the Indians' old weirs and spruce root traps were industrialized with numerous strategically placed large-scale traps and many bustling canneries serving distant markets.

Fish traps were elaborate, coast-hugging affairs which intercepted the salmon as they returned to the rivers and creeks of their birth. So profitable were the piling and net barriers that each had its own watchman to guard against fish pirate boats, the most notorious of which was the Spider.

Bert's double-ender was "a long slim fella that could slip through those seas just like nothin' to it." Equipped with a newfangled underwater muffler for silence, the 42-foot Spider was a frequent night caller at traps in all the complex maze of islands, shoals, straits, coves, and estuaries between Puget Sound and the Canadian border. "Spider" Jones's preferred method of operation was to rendezvous with a bribeable watchman according to a prearranged code. But when that was impossible he was always ready to raid traps on moonless nights or during fierce Pacific storms. In another time and place his encyclopedic coastal knowledge might have brought him honors as a Navy captain instead of notoriety as a fish pirate and bootlegger.

In 1934 Washington State banned the fish traps (which had often operated out of as well as in season) in order to conserve the dwindling fishery. That conservation measure (and the almost simultaneous repeal of Prohibition) made an honest fisherman of Spider Jones.

The battle of survival, especially illegal survival, might as well be fought with as much panache as possible. Bert Jones maintains that he was no more a crook than the trap owners themselves who were ruining the fish runs with their greed. In addition to his obvious skill, Spider was a proud and rather gentlemanly pirate. Although he was once mistaken for murderous Black Moon Pete who did fit the stereotype of a walk-the-plank pirate, this fish filcher carried no weapons and relied solely on superior cunning and speed. After years of legitimate fishing, Bert Jones finally abandoned his beloved but decrepit corsair on a rocky island where it broke to pieces.

Today, far from having regrets about his youthful depredations, Spider speaks passionately in favor of bringing back the fish traps as a needed source of jobs and food for the country. And just as passionately he dreams of having a new boat with which he would keep the fish trap operators honest.

Oh gosh, I used to be a crook. But I wasn't any more crooked than they were. They fished their traps during the closed season and were just as bad as me. Anyway, there were lots of fellas rustling fish, you know, but I was the only one who could make it pay. I used to get a load of fish every night. Oh yeah, I was suspected all the time. I had to slip it over on 'em. Oh golly, I used to have a lot of fun! Yes sir! Everybody in Anacortes knew I was a fish pirate. They called me Fish Pirate Jones. I didn't care what they called me just so I was making the money.

When the fish went into the trap's spiller, which was a big tarred web, the watchman closed the entrance tunnel and four men on a scow lifted that spiller up by hand and poured out the fish. I've seen a ten-foot-high spiller so full of humpback salmon that all the lifting crew had to do was start to brailing. They didn't have to lift the web at all. They put a big scoop down in there and let it sink. Then up they'd come with it plumb full of fish and put 'em over in the scow. Then drop her down again. A whole skowload of fish in one trap! Thousands of fish. Oh, I used to fill the Spider right up till the decks was under water. Boy oh boy! Oh, it was easy! I dropped a sack in there, pulled it up on my boat, and started to brailing. Gosh, I don't believe it would take me more than a quarter of an hour to load my boat.

Salmon got up to about seventy-five cents apiece. You were really into money when you got a boatload, say about two thousand fish.

The Spider was a forty-two-foot-long double-ender. My first engine was an old one-lunger clunk—but reliable. I started it with a tank of compressed air. I'd just turn her over and away we'd go. Poppity-pop. Poppity-pop. Gosh sakes, I'd open that thing up. Out comes cinders and everything. They'd go down the back of your neck. See, this big cylinder would coat over with soot which pretty soon started to break loose. If you was standing outside, why that stuff would still be afire blowing out of the chimney. I could set that engine so every pop would shoot up a smoke ring about that big.

I had other engines, too, but they wasn't very reliable. Once I was over at Guemes and had to tow the Spider back with a skiff. So I got rid of that engine in a hurry and put a diesel in. Boy, that was a dandy. It rolled over bang, bang, bang, bang just like clockwork. Four cylinders and boy she turned the old propeller to beat anything. I could sure travel! Boy, there wasn't any of 'em could keep up with me when I hooked her on. You bet! And I hooked her on many times, believe me! God damn, she was fast. I'd leave any boat that ever come alongside of me.

I kicked myself a long time for destroying the boat instead of fixing it up. It was leaking along the keel and I figured it was too old. She had a bad name, of course, but that didn't make no difference. By golly, I had the best of everything. Copper shaft and all so nothing would rust. Gee

whizzikers, that was a dandy. I should have fixed her up but, oh gee God, I took her over to Guemes Island and let her pound to pieces on the beach. That was a good boat!

I surely made money with that bugger. Often I'd take the fish while the watchman was asleep. Once I hit a trap fixed up with an alarm line and the watchman came running out and I had to go fast. But goldarn it, I went back and snipped that little line and made a clean sweep of his fish.

The owners had boats to patrol the traps and catch you if you got in. So I run up to one trap and asked, Do you have any fish to let go of? "Yes," he says, "but you better watch out. The patrol boat is running back and forth. Go down there and wait and I'll flash a light. Then you come running and I'll have the web down and all ready. All you'll have to do is throw your net in and make a scoop and drag 'em out. Then I'll up with the web and you can drift off." Well, after I was clear from the trap they had nothing on me at all.

I paid watchmen a hundred dollars or as high as six and seven hundred dollars for a load of fish. I used to take lots of money with me.

I had all kinds of codes. Someone would call and say, "Come on down to Long Island. We've got some rabbits here. Come on down and maybe we'll catch some." I says, All right, I'll be right down there and we'll have some fun.

You know, I could set right here in this house and I'd know where I'd get my next load of salmon. The phone would ring and the watchman would say, "If you want to see this engine, come on down now. I got this shed open and it's all ready." That was the signal to come to get a load of fish at Whidbey Island. Oh I had some great codes!

I had so many calls to come and get fish that I couldn't take care of them all. The watchmen figured the fish were made for everybody and they wanted their share. Everybody wanted to make money. The watchmen got paid for watching the traps and they got paid for selling the fish. They was killing two birds with one stone.

Gee whizzikers, I've sold tons of fish! The decks would be clear under water. I could sell all the fish I could get to the fish buyers who came out in their boats to buy from the purse seiners. They knew mine were fresh.

But a purse seiner will catch a hundred fish and not bother to find a fish buyer right away. He'll keep the fish for a couple of days and them fish'll be rotten when they get to the cannery. But they'd can them just the same.

The fish buyers looked for me every time because they knew I had fresh fish. They'd come alongside where I was layin' in the bay and I'd pitch 'em aboard. Nothing to it. Oh, they knew about me! ''We don't want to miss Pirate Jones,'' they'd say. ''He's got the fish.''

Oh boy, I had lots of fun! I'd go out when it got dark or when it got good and rough. I've been out there when it was so rough that some of the traps was tore out and all piled up on the shore. You could pick up oars and all kinds of stuff on the beach after one of those storms. But I was out there laying broadside to the traps, getting fish.

I run without lights altogether. I wouldn't run onto no rocks because I knew where to go. That was the easiest part. I'd look up in the sky. Or to get to a trap on a reef way out in the middle out there I used to follow the skags [cormorants]. The skags'd fly straight out to the fish trap. No matter how foggy it was, all I'd do was follow the skags. Nothin' to it. Big black birds. I had lots of tricks.

I'd keep hid during the day and come out during the evening after the patrol boats had all left. The nighttime was when I done my work, and they done theirs in the daytime. Gosh, I used to travel all over. Oh, the fish traps was thick. God, they were thick. Every night I used to get a load of fish.

There was a little place on Cattle Point where the patrol boats couldn't see me because I was laying up on the bank under the trees and brush. The watchman on the trap on the other side of the hill would walk over to tell me when to come for his fish. It was just a narrow little place. But an old guy started a farm there. God, I don't see how he could raise anything. There's nothing but rocks. You'd have to dig them rocks all out and then there wouldn't be dirt enough to cover a spud. But, by golly, he was a-digging away when I was there last. Didn't even want me to tie up.

Oh Jesus, I used to have whiskey all the time because I knew all the shallow water and rocks near the border. I had a pretty good setup at a fish trap clear up in Boundary Bay. The watchman'd go ashore in Canada and get some whiskey and bring it out to the trap. Then he'd put a note on the pile at the end of the lead, "Come about eight o'clock and get a load of cases of whiskey."

For a long time they was after me and wondering where I was getting my whiskey. But they never found out. Oh, I was a tough hombre. I peddled it around town. Oh gosh, I could make three, four, or five dollars a bottle.

I'd like to see the fish traps come back along with a law that would work. Traps are the best way to catch fish and can them. The fish are all the same age when they get to the cannery.

I'd like to see the fish traps come back because that puts many people to work. See, you go in the woods and cut them big pilings a hundred feet long and take 'em out to make the fish trap. That cutting and pile driving puts men to work. Then you buy the wire web which puts men to work, too. And the tarred web and the spiller. All of it puts men to work to catch these fish. As far as I'm concerned I don't care if I never get another fish, but I'd like to see the fish traps come back because they put so many people to work.

If they had protected the fish back then, we would have plenty now. Gee whizzikers, I have seen sockeyes so thick out in the bay at Cherry Point that there was nothing but splashing everywhere you looked. They all come up at the same time, flipping along, ten thousand in the school. I wasn't no distance from 'em at all. They all come up at once, then down they go and you never see 'em anymore. They keep right on a-going for the spawning grounds.

I say put the traps back and the first man that breaks the law, take his trap's spiller off and burn it on the beach. He wouldn't be stealing fish again that season.

As long as they didn't break the law, I wouldn't either. But if they start to steal the fish out of season, I'll have a little hand in it myself. By God, I used to get 'em!

13

Andy Dick

Canoemaker

Between the Strait of Georgia and the Strait of Juan de Fuca the Northwest coast sheers off into a maze of islands. Most are mere reefs or islets, spots for a cormorant or a gull to perch. Others, notably Vancouver Island and Whidbey Island, are bigger than many countries. Two hundred years ago explorers such as British Navy Captain George Vancouver and his sailing master Joseph Whidbey were amazed at the size and richness of this archipelago, all of which was up for grabs. Curiously, the two great islands which bear these comrades' names fly different flags because of a long-forgotten opéra-bouffe imbroglio known as the Pig War.

In the 1840's and 1850's, British and American settlers began to exploit the Oregon Territory's fisheries, farmland, forests, and minerals. But which nation would own all this wealth? The coast's highly developed but fratricidal Indian tribes enjoyed a brief artistic renaissance as a result of the introduction of iron tools, but their culture faded rapidly into a heritage of despair. The British claim to the region was solidly based on exploration and fur trading. And the Americans justified their cry of "54°40' or fight" on grounds of Manifest Destiny. For several decades everyone had to try to live amicably together without benefit of national sovereignty.

Finally in 1859 an American on disputed San Juan Island shot a British pig which was rooting in his potato patch. The animal's English owner demanded that the Yankee be brought to trial in the British Columbia provincial capital of Victoria. To protect this American citizen, the U.S. Army sent troops to the island. The British quickly countered with three warships. Fortunately no shots were fired by these Gilbert and Sullivan garrisons. The border issue was arbitrated in 1872 by Kaiser Wilhelm I in favor of the United States.

In spite of the region's political division, its primitiveness ensured a sort of natural unity until imported patterns of transportation, law, and trade could take hold. For instance, Etta Egeland of San Juan Island told me of sailing with her father in a small boat across the international frontier to Victoria to attend the birthday celebration for visiting Queen Victoria. Today only one group of people, the Indians, consistently maintains the old ties across the waters.

Each summer weekend Indian tribes compete in dugout races, their paddles striking in unison, voices chanting, and carved bows slipping gracefully through the water. Very often several of the six- or eleven-man canoes in a race will have been built by Andy Dick of the Chemainus Band of Coast Salish Indians on Vancouver Island.

Andy Dick's full head of dark hair belies his sixty-five years. He comes across as a kindly grandfather concerned about passing on his skills to his band's teenagers. I sensed that the canoes were much more to him than mere boats. He proudly remembered bowing and sailing long distances with his canoemaker grandfather in the '20's to obtain special rocks which would not crack in a fire. They were used to sear out the inside of a log canoe. "He was still doing it that way when I was fourteen years old," said Andy in heavily accented English. "It was slow, but it worked." From that experience to Andy's thirty-five-year career in a Seattle shipyard must have been quite a jump, though perhaps not as difficult as returning to recapture what he had known as a boy. Yet Andy Dick is succeeding.

Grandpa used to build me a trolling dugout whenever I needed one. After grandpa was gone my father showed me just once how to build a canoe. "You can do the rest," he said. So I didn't know much about it but I chopped up one anyhow. I used that one until it broke. Then I turned around and I got me another log and I built another one. I was just a kid.

And that was hard times, you know. That was chopping it with an axe all the way through. All I had was an axe, an adze, and a crosscut bucking saw. Two men were needed for the bucking saw. As for building a canoe, I was all by myself then. I chopped and tapered the ends with the axe. Then after the inside was dug out with the axe and adze I had to smooth the inside and the outside with a drawknife. I never used no planer, just a drawknife. Everybody said, "That's too much work. It takes too much time." But I went on. I worked, I worked, I worked until it was done.

For an eleven-man canoe I find a good red cedar tree, about five feet around. That's going to make a fifty-foot canoe. Sometimes if you want to make a six-man you get one good-sized tree and you split it in half and make two canoes out of it. I fall it myself and measure it to the length I want and rough it into shape. Then the boys come along with a cat and yard it out onto the road.

What I look for in a tree is how high the first limb is. If it's high enough, I take that tree for a canoe because there'll be hardly any knots. Some people see a tree with a clear side and say, "That's the bottom of my canoe." But the south side of a tree can be much lighter than the north side. If you split it from north to south, you can get a canoe that leans in the water.

I'll tell you the truth, all these canoes were just built by eye. There was no compass. There was no chalk line. Nothing to use at that time. You can build it by looking at it, that's all. You have to have a good eye. You could see both ends of your canoe. Maybe one part is bent a little too far. You can straighten it out.

You gotta make holes in the bottom to know how thick it is. They used to drill them out with a hot iron. Hell, now I got myself an electric drill and I make those half a dozen holes in not even a minute.

16

After the canoe is done we go out in the woods for pitch. You get a big bunch of pitch and you jack up both ends of the canoe, up high. And then you make a fire in something and you run that fire under there until the canoe's just black. Burn, burn, you burn the canoe with pitch. If you don't do that, it's going to crack when the sun hits it. The pitch cures the cedar and takes the moisture out. You can't burn it with just ordinary kindling wood. Pitch burns, flames up really nice. When you burn cedar you can hear it cracking. Well, that's the sound that you're gonna get until she's done and there's no more cracking anyplace.

I cure my canoes with dogfish liver oil. Then they never crack. For a few days they stink but then that smell goes away for good.

After awhile the canoes wear out, like if you were dragging it back and forth on the beach on barnacles and rocks when the tide is too far out. So one day we turn the canoe upside down on the beach to dry it out. The bottom is all raggedy from being dragged back and forth. So we burn it with the pitch again to make it lighter to pull with the oars. We use oars and oarlocks now for fishing, but they paddle the racing canoes. Anyway, that burning smooths out all that raggedyness. Then brush it over. And it's easier to row.

We leave enough wood in the bottom for wear but after four or five years she's all played out and can't be repaired anymore. So you throw it away and build yourself a new one.

It was very hard to build a canoe in the old days. But you have faith in something you really want to build. And you're gonna get it done. But if you only half wish, what's the use of trying it? If you're just thinking, I wonder if I could make that, I wonder, and then you try to make it, you wouldn't go very far. You'd quit with maybe just a half canoe laying there. That's what they call a bush canoe. You go and fall yourself a cedar and make it look like a canoe. Then you quit. They call it a bush canoe 'cause it's gonna stay up there in the bush.

The olden-time people, if they built something, they'd keep on building till they was through with it. But right now, these young people. Well, you can almost build yourself a canoe in one day with all these power tools. And still they can't build it themselves. It's hard to find one boy

17

interested in building a canoe. But the band chief and council here is going to get together to make those boys work. I'll show 'em how to do it, then watch 'em. If they're doing good, well, MacMillan Logging Company's gonna bring down a log and the boys are gonna build themselves a canoe. I'm just gonna show 'em once and they're gonna have to put it in their head, and build it, like the way I did myself when I was seventeen.

Grandpa always wanted me to be down there watching how to do it but I never had no time to go sit beside him when he was building a canoe. When I was a boy like my grandson I would sooner be out doing something else. Then after he was gone and I wanted a canoe I didn't have him no more. I asked my dad but he said, ''If you want a canoe, you're gonna have to build it yourself.'' Now I thank him for that. Otherwise I wouldn't have learned how to build. Then I thought he was mean to me. But I found out he was right.

Signe Ashland

"I always fished by myself"

Signe Ashland remembers hooking a 51-pound Skagit Bay salmon which almost pulled her overboard. Normally, however, she gill- netted, not hand-lined, from her 30-foot rowboat. Normal to her would spell arduous to many other people.

At 86, this thick-spectacled, frail-looking woman lives quietly in a nursing home in Mount Vernon, Washington, close to the Skagit River, scene of her independent life as a fisherwoman.

From her arrival alone in 1910 to her many decades of solitary fishing, Signe Ashland "made good at it." She is proud of the fish she caught and of her ability to finance numerous trips back to Sweden with her earnings. Her sight, hearing, and mobility are failing, but her enthusiasm remains undiminished. She beams like a schoolgirl when she recalls her 1910 trip to America, to "heaven," and the thought of a fresh-smoked spring salmon produces a burst of sudden strength in her weak body.

Some work is not work at all but the tide which carries a special person through life.

I always fished by myself, except sometimes my children would come and set with me. I did it for thirty years. That was my life.

When they outlawed our fish trap, then we got nets, the both of us. My husband Gunnar and I tried to beat each other. I caught more fish than he did many times, and he beat me many times, too.

There was a certain stretch where we were allowed to fish. You go up to Bald Island, throw out your net over a roller on the back of the rowboat, and drift down to the Goat Island jetty. Then pull up the net and row to Bald Island again. Lay out the net and drift down. That's the way we fished, following the tides. Sometimes you get on a slack, they call it, for three or four hours. If you don't learn the tides, it can leave you high and dry. Many times I'd fish too long and then I'd have to sit there. But I had things to do like cook some coffee until high tide. It wasn't so bad.

I used to fish nights 'cause the fish don't see the net then. Sometimes I'd start at eight or nine o'clock and drift with the tides all night. Once in a while I'd see a whale at night but not often because the fishermen killed them. If whales got in the net, they broke it to pieces. But I never killed them. Oh, they were the most beautiful things!

In the old days there was many fishermen because there were lots more fish. Off Bald Island it was all Swedes and Norwegians and Indians.

In 1910 I came by myself from Sundsvall in northern Sweden when I was just fifteen years old. Gunnar was cousin to all of us, and when he was home to Sweden one day I was cooking and washing the dishes and Gunnar tapped my dad on the shoulder. He said, ''This is the one I want. Don't give her away.''

So later when he sent for me I went to Sundsvall to buy clothes and a ticket. And then, oh my, I was on the way to heaven!

Lots of people rowed then or used dugout canoes because there wasn't very many motors. Took us two days to row north from Everett because it blowed hard southeast. I said, Let's go ashore. So we pulled the boat up and made supper. In the morning when we woke up we found we had slept in an old Indian cemetery with lots of tombstones they had made themselves of wood and cement.

But I got old. And my husband, he said, ''Oh, you quit that fishing.'' But he passed away and I'm all alone now. Looking for a new husband, but there are no fishermen left. They're all gone.

21

Well, I haven't given it up yet. I made good at it and now I'd get a new net and fish the river again.

I'd go out and get a few spring salmon. I'd clean 'em and cut 'em in slices and keep 'em in salt water for just one hour. Then hang them in the smokehouse with an alder fire. Alder makes the best taste. I like fresh smoked fish best. I'd cut it in slices, dip it in egg, and fry it. Put pepper and salt. That's good!

Yes, we worked hard. It took some muscle to pull the net in. I had to learn to be strong. But it's not difficult at all if you like it. When I lived in the old country I used to row and fish there, too, when I was growing up. Oh, it was fun. If you have it in you when you're growing up, you can't get away from it when you get older.

Mark Gilkey

Skagit River Gambler

Ninety-five-year-old Mark Gilkey's white hair, courteous manner, and string-tie elegance belie his Huckleberry Finn-like youth on Samish Bay. Or his career seventy years ago running a professional poker game in the Skagit River's wild mining and logging towns.

Eventually Mark Gilkey became a successful tugboat company owner plying the inland waters of Washington state.

My granddad took up a homestead right across from the town of Edison. He had to dike about two-thirds of it against the salt water to raise timothy hay. I was born in Edison on a clam bed on Samish Bay.

There was quite a number of Indian canoes. You see, the Indians depended a good deal on the saltchuck [salt water] for clams, oysters, and salmon for their living. I even remember seeing the big war canoes of the northern Indians when they would come down here. Big high prows on 'em with a little face figure.

As a boy I started my navigating in a little shovel-nosed canoe in Edison Slough. At one time it was the North Fork of the Samish River until the loggers dammed it off and turned all the water down the South Fork so they could float their logs down to the salt water where they could boom 'em up for towing. The North Fork became a tidewater slough then.

A shovelnose is a river canoe. The others are sharp-bowed and if the current catches them it'll slue 'em . But the shovelnose'll go right up against the current and won't be slued around. I used to steal the Indians' dugouts and their paddles. They always knew it was me, and then Mother would trim me for it.

I learned how to find where their paddle caches were. They'd cache them in thick evergreen trees. Bundle them all up and shove them way up in there. I got onto that. I'd pull that down, then shove a canoe off the bank if it wasn't too big. I just wanted something to ride in.

A few years later I had a gas cruiser, the Hiawatha. Her engine was built in Seattle at N & S—Noise and Stink we called it. But it was a reliable old engine. I'd been with a gang over at Anacortes liquoring up, you know, and when we were coming home in my boat in the middle of the night, why, we decided we were going to blow up the Edison Jail. Because they had built it for just one particular drunkard. He wasn't in it at the time.

A cousin of mine and one or two others were clearing land up at the east end of Edison. Clearing timber and blowing up stumps on a farm there. So it was all framed up as we come from Anacortes that they would walk to their dynamite cache and bring it down and blow the jail up. As an alibi I was not supposed to come steaming up into town with the boat until afterwards.

When I first got up there here was the postmaster and the town constable and some others standing there looking at the wreck. It was evident that I was mixed up in it because I come steaming up to my dock right near the jail just after the explosion. Later on the county sheriff come over to quiz me. I told him, well, as I came into the slough in the middle of the night another vessel, a little gas boat, passed me going out. And, I said, he was operating without running lights. So I didn't know who it was. And the sheriff couldn't pin anything on me.

I started gambling as just a young kid. We'd sneak around to play in the loft in the barn. I guess I was just a little crook at heart. As I look back on it now I must have been.

When I was in my early twenties I ran a poker game in the town of Concrete. They had two big cement plants there then, and it was a hot town. A live wire town! All those workmen, you know. Loggers in their bright mackinaws, what we called squaw-catchers because the Indian women liked them so much. Plenty of tinhorns and sporting women and their macs.

There were two or three hotels and a lot of saloons and sporting houses. Nell's, for instance. She had this vaudeville actor pimp, Ronnie McCarty. Sometimes he'd tend bar, too. One night in one saloon I raked off $125 and never turned a card. I took a rake-off offa' the pot, see. But, of course, I bought the drinks. Every so often the players could have all the drinks they wanted.

Oh, you had to have a bankroll to handle a card game! I always ran an open blackjack game. No limits! Anybody with a lot of money could come in and tap your whole bankroll. You don't see that anymore. They have a limit on their games now. I shoulda had a limit, too, if I'da had any brains. One time in another town a fella tapped me in blackjack and I went broke.

In the average small town there were usually only one or two games. In Concrete I had the only game. I made good money.

One time I had to carry a gun because a fella from Bellingham was going to get noisome, as it were. I carried a gun against him because I was terribly sick at that time. Just couldn't even hold a soda water on my stomach. I was dealing at that time, and I would have shot the bugger if he had ever tangled with me because he was a big burly guy and he could have killed me. The only sheriff was down at the county seat in Mount Vernon.

Cheating was another problem sometimes. There's a dozen ways, like marking cards with your fingernails, cold decking, invisible numbers, rings with little mirrors on them. But if you were a real dealer, you never allowed monkeywork in your game. If you saw a man working, you reached over and took his chips away from him. He was out. You'd never even speak.

He knew the score. No, we never allowed any crookedness.

Finally one of the cement plants quit and the town went flat. Then I went upstream to Marblemount with another gambler and started gambling there. But I got disgusted with it. As a matter of fact, I really got ashamed of myself. I thought, well, you're a nice pill trying to cheat people around here out of their money. I really got ashamed of myself thinking I was making a living in that kind of a deal. I felt sorry for the men who worked hard for their money. Even the married men used to soak their watches to me to get money to carry on with the card game. One fella even soaked his wife's watch for more chips.

So I quit cold! I got fed up on it. I had a change of heart, in other words.

Bill Robler

"Swing her around like swinging on a gate"

Old-time wrangler and lifelong Methow Valley resident Bill Robler was a noted bullhorn announcer at area rodeos in pre-microphone days. His robust voice also made him a popular quadrille caller. Quadrilles are four-couple dances in which (unlike square dancing) only one couple at a time is moving through the pattern. Some of his favorites are "Captain Jinks" and "Dig for the oyster, dive for the clam, dive for the sardine, get a full can."

Bill Robler is not happy with today's "commercialized" style of living and loves to tell how he and his neighbors used to share what little they had up on "Poverty Flats."

W hen I got to be sixteen I could drive the U.S. mail. I had to hold up my right hand and swear to protect Uncle Sam's mail. Granddaddy, Joe Barcelou, ran that stage for years beginning in 1909. Just a team and hack and, in the winter, a sled. He wasn't afraid of no man, beast, or the devil, I don't think.

We had to stop at the mail posts and the horses got so's they'd know these stopping places. When they got rested they'd move on. And we hauled passengers, too. Four bits to go from Pearl to Bridgeport and a dollar for the twenty-four-mile round trip.

I learned quadrilles close to sixty years ago from an old guy from Kentucky who ran the Pearl store. He said, "By God, your voice'll carry."

Say, would you like me to call a little for you?

First couple balance and swing, and down the center and divide the ring. Lady go right and gent go left. Swing and you meet both head and the feet, and the same as you did before, and down the center and cast off four. Lady go right and gent go left. Swing and you meet both head and the feet. Do the same as you used to do, and down the center and cast off two, and lady go right and gent go left. Swing and you meet. Everybody swing. Corner swing. Now you're home if you're not too late. Swing her around like swinging on a gate. Second couple balance and swing. And down the center, divide the ring. Lady go right and gent go left. Swing and you meet both head and the feet. And do the same as you did before, down the center and cast off four. Lady go right and gent go left. Swing and you meet both head and the feet. Do the same as you used to do, down the center and cast off two. Lady go right and gent go left. Swing and you meet both head and the feet. Everybody swing. Allemande left. Allemande left. Allemande left. And a left allemande. Hand over hand. Right and left red. Hurry up boys and away you go. And meet your partner, a double elbow. Hook and a keep a-hookin' on.

Oh, there are all kinda calls.

You know, I gotta tell you a story about Ole Scott. In the old days everybody trusted everybody because there was no need for mistrust. Well, a neighbor across the way from me was cultivating with a one-horse cultivator. I had a little corn so I went to see him. I says, How's the chance to use your cultivator? "Well," he says, "we got it from Roy Carter, our son-in-law. You'll have to ask him."

I did and he said, "Well, it ain't mine. You'll have to ask Boy Divers."

Well, I went up and saw Boy. How's the chance to use your cultivator when you're done with it? I asked.

"Well, you'll have to see Ole Scott. I got it from him." So I went to Scott's. Hey, Ole, I says, how's chances to borrow your cultivator?

Ole said, "God, have I got one? I don't know. If I've got one," he says, "you can borrow it."

Then someone said, "Hell, Scott, that's the one you borrowed from Bill three years ago."

And it was! I was trying to borrow my own cultivator from all the neighbors. I'd forgotten where mine was. Well, Ole might have come down and borrowed it when I was gone. He knew it was all right.

Deke Smith

"Crazy with fiddling"

Eighty-five-year-old Theodore "Deke" Smith of Smith Canyon spends a lot of time swatting flies and "jackets" and looking out the door of his one-room cabin at the sere Okanogan hills. Ponderosa pines straggle up the slopes like herds of cattle. I wish I could imagine Smith Canyon as he sees it. His father had homesteaded on this spot at the turn of the century. Deke has watched the elimination of the Indians, the salmon, the game, and then, through bank fore-closures during the Depression, many of the homesteaders (including himself). Even language has changed. Occasionally another old cowhand drops by and for fun they speak a little Chinook, which was the region's trade language when they were boys. Despite all of these changes, Deke today has neither electricity nor indoor plumbing. "I wouldn't know how to live in a modern house," he grins.

Actually, Deke's cabin is brand new; it was built recently by dozens of his young friends, most barely a third his age, who got together for an old-time house-raising. Reviving pioneer traditions of neighborliness, they held a dance benefit, donated materials, and volunteered construction labor.

When I last visited the cabin, Deke was worried about his failing health. "I'm on my next to last switchback," he said matter-of-factly. But we soon "cinched down" to the business at hand and the stories started to come fast and free in that good, gruff storytelling voice which I hoped would never quit.

Actually, when I was a kid there were more Indians up here on the Methow than there were white people. This right in here used to be a great camping place for 'em in the summertime. There was deer hunting, and the squaws could come up for berries. In the fall they'd catch salmon here on Libby Creek with a little trap. I don't know how a salmon would get up this crick now. Not enough water for him to come up. I can still remember when my dad put in a trap right up there by the house. Oh, the salmon would just be a-boiling in there. A lot of them'd jump over, but he'd catch more'n a little bit.

There was an Indian camp above there a ways and they kinda resented his salmon trap. So, he was kind of a politician, so he told them he had a hell of a good salmon trap and more salmon than he could use. So why didn't they all use it? Then Indians'd come down and get their salmon, too.

But no Indian ever stayed here in winter. They were smarter than that. You'd never see an Indian shovelling snow.

Wintertime we were more or less snowbound but that didn't make no difference. People's gotta have company or they'll climb the walls. Families was all scattered out. So every Saturday night they'd hitch up the old sleighs. Of course, young guys had their saddle ponies and could make better time. People thought nothing of going out at ten below zero, maybe in a snowstorm, eight or ten miles through the snow to some house. The whole tribe'd go and wedge in there, Grandpa, Grandma, babies, and the whole works. They'd throw everything out but the stove and sometimes even that. At midnight they'd call a halt for a great feed. And if anybody had any booze, they'd drink. Hard cider used to be quite a thing.

Hoedowns! Missourians call 'em shirttail crackins. Others call 'em belly rubbins. In the early days that was our recreation.

I think we had better social life then. We're too much separated now. You take right up there in Twisp. OK, all them honky-tonks, barrooms

in other words, Saturday night they get a little music in there and everybody has a good time—except the teenagers. All right. Where have them teenagers got to go? There's no place for them to go. Not a show. No place to go to dance. So they take to the timber. Then they're outlaws, you see. So that's what I'm a-meowin' about now.

Do you remember *The Virginian*? That story was supposed to be in Wyoming, but Owen Wister put in a lot of things which actually happened here. Like that baby stealing, for instance. One time at a dance a couple of old curmudgeons went where the babies were sleeping and changed the blankets on them. These mothers, when the dance was over, way in the early morning, many below zero, they took their kids home. Just grabbed 'em up. That's my blanket; that's my baby. When they got home and uncovered them they had the wrong babies. Then they had to drive all that distance to trade babies.

Everybody had a fiddle, it seemed like. I often thought if we had old Uncle Bill, George Frederics, and old Uncle Pete Scott all here at the same time, they'd have run these Methow people crazy with fiddling. Old George Frederics was an old boy that lived over the hill there on the Davis place. And my old Uncle Bill used to play a pretty wicked fiddle. Of course, that's all they had then. Some old boy might have a banjo but that was quite an oddity. What I don't like now is that a fiddle, he's pretty near out. They've gone guitar-happy.

Oh, and they had a scroungy old fella, old Arkansas. His real name was A.C. Brannon. But he went by the name of Arkansas all his life, he said, because his prize tune was "The Arkansas Traveller." He could play it purty, so he got the name Arkansas. You've heard that old tune, haven't you?

I think he was hatched out someplace in the desert or off in a pine tree. He didn't know himself. Or if he did, he never told. He was an old-time buffalo hunter and fiddler. He went into the gold rush in California, but all he done was fiddle for his drinks and living. Finally he got tired of that and he packed up his saddle horse and his fiddle and wound up here.

He was a foul old booger. No haircut. I don't think he'd had one in fifty years. But he was always clean shaven.

His cabin was about five miles up the road above ours. He'd leave his fiddle with us and on Saturday afternoon here he'd come to retrieve it to go out to play for a dance. They'd take up a collection and maybe sometimes he'd get as much as a dollar. That's what he lived on. That and his rifle and traps. Finally he got so old they give him up as a fiddler and he couldn't hunt no more and he was starving to death. That's what ailed him. Starvation and old age. Nobody knew how old he was. He didn't know himself.

Finally, when he was dying, another old boy, Booth, who lived at the mouth of Booth Canyon, he was a pretty clean old bachelor, ''Hell,'' he says, ''Ark, I'm gonna give you a bath.''

''Oh my God,'' Ark says, ''Booth, don't do it. It'll kill me sure. I haven't had a bath in thirty years.''

''OK, but you're gonna get it anyway.''

So Booth put Ark in a tub and scrubbed him up and put him to bed. Next morning old Arkansas was deader'n a nit.

Well, he didn't have dime one. And everybody else around, they was poor as the devil. So they took up a collection among the neighbors. Nickels and dimes. They got up to two dollars, and the old merchant uptown, he picked up the rest and give 'em a blanket for that. So they wrapped old Ark in the blanket and laid him low.

Ralph Parker

Tarheel Moonshiner

For generations the manufacture of moonshine, homemade untaxed alcohol, has been an essential part of one kind of rural ecomonic survival. It was so important two centuries ago that western Pennsylvania farmers took up arms in the 1794 Whiskey Rebellion against the new federal government's attempts to tax their easily-transported liquid corn. Today the fiery drink is made by more sophisticated equipment and its makers apprehended by ever more ingenious devices. Ironically, as the energy crisis worsens the U.S. government may begin to promote home distilling—for gasohol.

The Prohibition Era was moonshine's heyday, and the Southern Appalachians its capital. Carolina Tarheel Ralph "Stogie" Parker began his career as a master moonshiner in the 1920's because, he says, that was the only way many mountain men knew to feed their families.

Stogie moved to Lyman, Washington, at the beginning of World War II and became a logger. He and many other Carolina immigrants brought with them an Appalachian thirst for moonshine not easily satisfied in the Northwest. For awhile Stogie helped to meet that demand. But after his arrest a few years ago he switched to raising hounds and vegetables. Now, at 74, if he wants some of the heady drink in the Mason jar, he has to buy it from somebody else.

Ralph Parker is a stocky, intense man whose descriptions of old feuds, murders, and battles with the "high sheriff" are delivered with a burning flame of enmity quite unknown in TV comedy versions of this popular subject. For some in the '20's moonshine meant survival—and it was not a laughing matter to people like Ralph Parker.

I tell you, you can make lots of money here in logging work, but if you've got a little farm back in Carolina, you can live better than here.

I make enough in my garden now to feed three families. Of course, I go to the store and buy what I want, but I'd rather have stuff like I was raised on. Beans. Peas. Carrots. I've got that whole garden planted in 'em.

We made an easier living back in the '20's than we do now. Now whiskey's twenty-five dollars a gallon and the most you could get for it then was four dollars. But you could buy all the sugar you wanted then for thirty cents a pound. I could buy more with five dollars then than you can buy with fifty right now. Another thing, living back in them hills, we didn't need no money to amount to nothin'. Sugar. Flour. And coffee. The rest of it we growed. I've seen times when we had five hundred head of hogs running loose in the woods. Cattle and sheep. And them bear was better'n beef.

Three of us went to making whiskey in '25. But a lot of the time I was by myself. That's the way we fed our families through the Depression. There wasn't nothin' else to do then. No money and no way to get none.

In Jackson County, North Carolina, Sylva was the big town, the county seat. Our post office was Rich Mountain. The guy who had the store down on the river would bring me all my sugar and corn, groceries, whatever I needed, and take whiskey to pay for it. Then he resold it, of course. And I'd sell a gallon here and there to fellas passing by.

Carolina whiskey has a bead on it like a bird's eye. A bubble that stays right around the edge of the jar. The corn is what makes the bead. In a fifty-gallon barrel we put a half bushel of corn meal and half a bushel of sprouted, ground-up corn malt. And we'd put a half bushel of rye in there to cap it. Then put fifty pound of sugar and you'll get about eleven, twelve gallon of whiskey out of a fifty-gallon barrel.

Corn and sugar and rye. We made the beer in a barrel, then run it through a copper still for about thirty-six hours. Build a wood fire in the furnace and boil it till nothing but whiskey come out. Hundred and forty and eighty proof. Then we'd proof it down to about a hundred proof to drink it.

We'd run two runs a week. One about Tuesday and on Friday night. And we'd get anywhere from eleven to fourteen gallon out of a fifty-gallon barrel of beer. It finally went up to four dollars a gallon.

I run them revenooers a lotta races. They cut down my still one time. But I got away and they couldn't catch me. I was used to follering them hound dogs, so I was fast. When they busted it up I had two barrels of beer. But I was gone before they got there. A guy told me they was gonna raid it. Later they come by with that still on their backs. I knowed that high sheriff. He was a blockader and a bootlegger till he got in as sheriff. He said, ''If anybody claims this, I'll give it to 'im.'' I said, Bill, you're a smart sonofabitch, ain't ya? They had an idea it was mine, but they couldn't prove it.

Back then I didn't go nowhere 'cause it was twenty-one mile to town from where I lived. The post office was in a store just two mile below home. We made what we ate and we made what we wore. We had our own looms and spinning wheels. We had sheep and cattle. Pigs in the woods. And we bear hunted with a bunch of bear dogs. My dad was the greatest hunter in North Carolina. We'd kill lots of bear. They're good eating. And coons. Back there, ain't nothing better'n a coon to eat.

We was coon hunting and the high sheriff could see our lights on them hills. So he got to laying along the road where he figured we'd come down. That sonofabitch just thought that badge made him a king. We were walking down the highway with two coons and he jumped out on us and I beat hell out of him and throwed his gun away. He took us to court and I beat him 'cause he'd caught us on the state highway. I told him if he ever came back around I'd kill him.

My first cousin Demos Woods, Gus was his nickname, and that sheriff had a still up there together. A big one—three hundred gallon. After he got to be sheriff Bill sent Gus word that he was coming out to cut their

still down. Gus told him, "You're in Sylva now. You stay down there and run that, and I'll run this up here." So Bill went out there one Sunday and sent a deputy sheriff to ask Gus to come down the road and talk to him. But Gus knowed him and knowed he was dirty. He said he got to studying it and got his shotgun and went around the back where he could see around the curve. He saw the sheriff sitting there with a .30-30 across his lap waiting for him to come down the road. So Gus shot his head off and rolled him off the road. Then he took off and they hunted for him.

Well, he had ten gallon of whiskey buried there at his shack. They had a bench warrant for him and he said he knowed they'd get him. He sneaked in there one evening, opened up that keg and drunk just as long as he could drink a drop. They found him laying on the porch passed out. He told the judge, "I knowed that was the only way I'd ever get to town alive." Well, they gave him thirty years. That was in '29, I believe.

Five revenooers were sent into the mountains one time to a place they called Nigger Skull. Never did find 'em. Then they sent in two detectives. Never did find them either. Revenooers wouldn't go back in there after that. Nothing but dead end roads, sled roads, horse roads, for thirty miles into town. Wasn't no cars. I had the first T-model that ever went up in there.

A lotta them old guys had never been to town. They wasn't mean, them sonofabitches. They was crazy. None of 'em ever went to school in their damn life.

In 1942 I was working for the state, driving a truck at Waynesville, North Carolina. They shut that down and wanted us all to go to Pearl Harbor. My boss man went and he tried to get me to go. But I wouldn't. My dad and brother was up here so I come here in place of going to Pearl Harbor, and I been here ever since.

I was logging fallen timber when I come out here. There was only Swedes here then, but us Tarheels took it over.

When I come here me and my brother went up there on the hill and got a half gallon from an old guy. I wouldn't drink it. Didn't have no bead on it like Carolina whiskey.

I couldn't drink the whiskey here. They made it out of bolted meal. That doesn't make good whiskey. Mill run was the name of it. It's corn meal that's been run through the mills. Bolted to keep it from molding or musting. They run it through some kind of presser and take the heart out of it. Takes all the strength out of it is what it does. Back in Carolina, if you get corn meal, it's pure stuff.

Oh, them guys made a lot of whiskey. They had a flood here one time and water was all over the place. Old Pinty Metcalf had a ten gallon keg of whiskey. Everybody was a-leaving town, and they went down after Pinty. He said, ''Wait, I ain't a-going till I get me one more drink.'' He poured him out a bottle out of that keg.

They got him up on the hill, but he slipped off and come back. He wasn't gonna leave his whiskey even though the water was coming right up in his house.

Making whiskey was all Pinty ever done, back up on that crick, our old watershed. We had the best water in the world here. It come out of them mountains. But that cottonpicker company, they logged it all off and we ain't got no more watershed. We get our water out of a pump now.

When I come here I'd quit fooling with whiskey but after I'd retired from logging I had nothing to do. Aw, it was easy money. That was the reason I was doing it. A guy come here to make whiskey and I showed him how. Hell, he was making good whiskey. Not that old mill run. He bought corn from east of the mountains.

He set up a still in an old cheese factory that had been abandoned for years. A big cement building. He used stainless steel cause it won't burn like copper. All automatic. He'd just turn it on in the morning and go off and leave it. At a certain temperature it'd shut itself off. He didn't have to be around there or nothing. When they raided his still he had twelve hundred gallon of beer and five hundred gallon of whiskey.

Well, I sold a lot of it. But I had two or three stool pigeons turning me in all the time here. A man would get drunk on wine and beer and these damn women would accuse him of buying moonshine. One time three women went to the sheriff to complain that their husbands were getting moonshine from me and staying drunk. Nary a one of 'em did buy any. One of 'em did steal a gallon once out of my briar patch. He tore that briar patch all to pieces and found that gallon I'd left in there. He stayed drunk for two or three days and that's where his wife got the idea I'd sold him moonshine. If I'da caught him, he'd still be in that briar patch.

And these tavern guys, they was knocking me. Said I was a-hurting their business. Two of them turned me in. That's how it got started, and it kept getting worse. It wound up there was six of them Federals hanging around here.

Well, I wouldn't sell nobody a drop here. Too close to home. Guys come from way off to get whiskey. But I just got too damn careless.

Two guys kept hanging around here. I told my partner, Dolan, a guy who was selling it with me, I told him they were FBI men. He didn't believe it. He was a goofy kind of a guy. He'd walk right up to a preacher in town and ask if he wanted to buy a gallon.

Dolan's truck was tore down, so he come and got mine and put five gallon in it. We went up the road to sell to those fellas who were waiting on us up there. When that undercover agent took the whiskey out of my truck he opened up the back of his old panel wagon and there was two more FBI men in there. They got out and one of 'em drawed a gun.

They throwed us in jail that night but I got out the next morning. Five hundred dollar bond.

I ain't gonna get in trouble with no more whiskey. I quit. I'm too old to fool with it. I ain't seen no moonshine since then. Nobody makes it anymore around here.

Gene Grush

Mulligan Stew

Eighty-five-year-old homesteader Gene Grush and his wife Ruth own the old townsite of Sylvanite, Montana. In 1910, when much of the northwestern part of the state was ablaze with monstrous forest fires, Sylvanite burned to the ground. That conflagration was what brought Gene Grush into the country. His arduous travels show an instinct for survival which has held him in good stead throughout his life.

I was born in Pittsburgh, Pennsylvania and lived there until I was fifteen. I probably shouldn't say it, but my mother was a tyrant. We were Catholics and she was going to insist that I be a priest. Well, I didn't have that idea myself! But I'd make my breakfast each morning and then I'd run two miles to the church and be altar boy to the priest and then I'd run a half mile back to get to school on time. Then at noon I had to run home and eat and run back again. By God, I should have been a marathon runner or entered the Olympics. Well, they didn't have Olympics that I knew of then. Anyway, then I'd have to pack the groceries home from the grocery store and hike way up the hill to get the cows for our landlord.

44

I took it as long as I could. Finally, just before my ▮
in March, when I was just about to graduate from grade ▮
off. I used to get a nickel a night for bringing the cows home▮
I had three dollars and seven cents saved up I took off and head▮

And I rode freight trains and I rode the blinds and I rode th▮
and I rode on top of them and I rode inside of them and I hiked. I coun▮
lots of ties. I worked my way. I washed dishes in a cafe in Battle Creek,
Michigan. And I worked in the harvest fields and farms in Kansas and
Nebraska. I worked in a sawmill in Dover, Idaho. And various other jobs
along the way. I'd split wood for people for a meal. I worked my way across
the country.

Conditions were rather difficult. I slept anywhere when I was coming across the country. I slept under doorsteps, and in coal bins, and in
freight cars. One time I had a newspaper I used for a blanket.

Back East you travelled light with only the clothes you had on you.
Then later, after I got out West here, you packed your own blanket. You
used to call it your bindle. A blanket, maybe a bar of soap, a straight razor,
and a towel rolled up with a piece of rope around it. That was it. We just
carried it under our arm. A hell of a lot different from today! You bet.
Nowadays you see them hiking and travelling along with a big aluminum
packsack that sticks clear up above their head.

I've got a Trapper Nelson packboard I used to use years ago. It was
made of wood and it had rings on it so you could use it by roping your
bundle or its packsack onto it. It had a little rod that run down through
these two rings to fasten the packsack on. That was a long time ago, but
it was a hell of a good outfit. Pretty deluxe for that time. If you had a Nelson,
you were somebody. Of course, there were the ordinary packsacks but that
Nelson was really something. You were in the elite if you had a Nelson.

I damn near got killed someplace in Michigan. I was sitting on this
bunch of ties waiting for a train to come along. When it did it wasn't stopping. I had learned to run alongside of a train before I grabbed onto a handle
to get on. And I did, but my hat blew off. And so I dropped off and I ran
back and I grabbed my hat and I shoved it in my jacket front and started
back for the train again. I looked and here was the caboose coming. So

aid the caboose was gonna get
ust grabbed it and it just threw
oss the rails. But with the shock
up like that. Anyway, the man
me and said, "My God, boy,
t across that rail, and I started
re you died." He said, "You
1 the tower and talked with
s from and what I was doing
…. And he gave me some good advice. He said,
you get on the steps behind the engine." In between the tender and the
baggage car was what they called the blind, enough space to stand where
they coupled together without standing on the couplings. "Two boys,"
he said, "got on the blind here awhile back. That train takes water on the
fly. They have a big trough in the middle of the tracks and they don't stop
to load up with water. They just put a scoop down and scoop the water
right back up into the tender. When they did that, those two boys didn't
realize what it was, and they both jumped and were killed. So," he said,
"you get back on the steps tonight. I'll tell the conductor that you'll be
on there!"

I remember stopping in one hobo jungle that was very popular. They
had a fifty-pound lard pail there. And they used to make stew in that lard
pail. They had an open fire with rocks around it to set the pail on. And
they'd have a wire on the coffee can so they could rig it to hang from sticks
over the fire. Those boys used to fix some pretty good food sometimes.
Mulligan stew. Hobo stew.

I never paid a damn cent for transportation until I got to Paradise near
Bozeman, Montana. We were riding in a refrigerator car. In those days
they used to have ice in one end of the car. But this one was empty. A bunch
of us got in. So many of us that we couldn't lie down or anything. We
were standing up. We got to Paradise and the town bull, the town cop,
come and he opened that up and said, "OK, boys, out you go." So we
all got out and stood there on the platform and then the train pulled out.
We went over to the hotel and had breakfast. And we watched the town

cop. Pretty soon he sauntered off. Then a Barnum and Bailey circus train come in and stopped at the depot. So we sauntered over there. We couldn't get into the cars, of course, so we looked around and underneath they had a kind of a platform on the rods. So we crawled onto that. The train stopped somewhere before we got to Sandpoint, Idaho, and here the brakeman come along. He was smartalecky. "OK, boys," he says. "Where you goin'?" Well, we thought maybe Sandpoint. "OK, that's gonna cost you two bits apiece," he said. So we shelled out the two bits. And that's the only time I had to pay to ride a freight.

How did I happen to come up to this part of the country? Well, when I got to Alliance, Nebraska, the line split there. One went north and the other went straight west. I didn't know which way to go. So I thought it over for awhile and I decided to take the first train that came along. So I did, and the first one was headed north.

I got to Spokane in August. By then this whole damn country was afire and they wanted men to fight it. So I hired out.

This area has changed a lot. When I first come in here the town had just burned and it was a mess of ashes. All these trees have grown up since. I grew up with 'em.

Al Coffelt

"Five cents an hour, ten hours a day"

Ninety-nine-year-old Al Coffelt is locally famous on San Juan Island for having had the island's first automobile, a tiller-steered Orient buckboard. Recently that car's restorer drove it in a parade with a beaming Al Coffelt as passenger.

But Al's most interesting memories predate the twentieth century to a period of severe economic depression. Out in the islands between the Strait of Georgia and the Strait of Juan de Fuca only the then-abundant sea kept many families from starving.

My father was born in Missouri where they used to have fever and ague. He told his folks, he says, "As soon as I'm old enough I'm gonna leave this country." Somewhere about 1870 he started out to walk west from Missouri. He finally got in with a freighting team and worked for them and made his way across. He got as far as Montana. Then he broke horses there for awhile. Finally when he got to the San Juan Islands there was no further to go.

We lived on Blakely Island where he built a water-powered sawmill. He framed that mill, built all the parts, the timbers, braces, and everything.

48

To hold the braces he'd bore a hole through the timbers and drive in wooden pins. There was no iron bolts around. Then they had a mill-raising. I guess everybody from all around the whole county was there. I remember I stood on the hill and looked down to see them. A lot of men hauling with block and tackle putting the mill up. They put it up in a day.

My father sold that mill. Practically give it away. People don't really know what hard times was. In Cleveland's administration there was no way to get any money. People worked for five cents an hour in the logging camps and sawmills. They had a store where they had to take their wages out in trade. Five cents an hour! Ten hours a day. And they worked, too!

We lived on Blakely at that time. We couldn't sell any lumber. There was no work. Years later one of my aunts asked one of my brothers about it. He said, ''All we had to eat was popcorn and ice.''

Most of the people raised their own food. I can remember when flour was sixty-five cents for a fifty-pound sack. A hundred pounds of sugar for two and a half. I can remember when there wasn't any white sugar. It was all brown sugar. People most all baked their own bread in cookstoves. Lots of biscuits. They raised lots of potatoes which they usually stored in a pit.

Farmers used to have what they called a seine boat. A double-ender about twenty-four feet long. Six feet wide. They'd take a whole load of potatoes, apples, or whatever they had to Bellingham in that rowboat. I went a couple of times with my uncle when he took a load of apples.

It would take all day to row to Bellingham. We had a sail and if there was any wind, why, we'd sail.

There wasn't much inland farms. Most everyone had a place on the waterfront where they'd raise a garden and put out an orchard. I can remember when there was no horses here. They did their plowing and everything with oxen. When they brought a horse here on a steamer they'd go up as close as they could get to the beach and push the horse overboard and let it swim ashore. I remember when I first started in school on Orcas, one day somebody came by with a horse and there almost was a riot to get to see that horse.

Of course, there was lots of salmon and fishermen caught them with

a plain cotton gill net. But there was no sale for any kind of fish but just the dogfish oil. In the summertime the dogfish fishermen would usually fish from a rowboat for dogfish, then dry out the livers and sell the oil. I think they got about fifteen cents a gallon.

To get money I used to build a V-bottom double-ender cedar rowboat for a dollar a foot. That was a lot of money at that time. My father taught me how to build 'em. He was a good workman. We'd go out and pick up drift logs. There were lots of nice cedars drifting around in those days. Booms would break up and the logs would go adrift. We'd take them to the sawmill to be made into boards, then plane them with a hand plane.

We used galvanized nails for boat work because they wouldn't rust. They were all square cut at that time.

We'd mix our own paint out of white lead and linseed oil and give them one coat. There was no filler or dryer or anything in it. Lots of boats never got painted because people didn't have the paint.

Dad hardly ever used oarlocks because a set cost twenty-five cents. He would put pins like they have in the Navy and save the twenty-five cents. Then we'd shape our oars out of a piece of cedar with a drawknife.

Oh, I built a good many boats. A boat was the only way to get around. There was a young man on San Juan Island who'd go over to Orcas Island on the passenger boat to visit a girl. But he had no way to come home Saturday night. He'd have to borrow a rowboat somehow to get back. Or stay over Sunday. Once he asked Mr. Cadwell for his daughter. Mr. Cadwell, who was quite hard of hearing, thought he was asking for the boat to get back to San Juan. He says, ''Oh yes, you can take her, but the Indians been draggin' her up and down the beach and she leaks pretty bad. But you can take her.''

But he didn't get the girl anyhow!

Later I worked on a fish trap on the south end of Lopez and we filled a forty-foot scow with salmon every day. And they got a cent and a half apiece for them. When sockeyes got to be sixteen cents apiece, that was a fortune.

Stanley Darwood

Ice Harvest

Stanley Darwood at ninety is a heavyset man who rarely strays far from his armchair. As he talks, however, his life of vigorous outdoor work sings through his stories. This hearty fellow gives the impression that if his body were willing he would be out there yet with the best of them.

Stanley immigrated to the United States from England in 1905, when he was sixteen years old. "It was all the go," he says jovially. "Canada, Australia, and America was all open for homesteads and the people was flocking in from all parts of Europe."

In 1921 Stanley settled down on a bend of the Methow River south of the village of Twisp in the Okanogan country. Because of its excellent location his place soon became the neighborhood center for a kind of winter work festival—the ice harvest. (Strangely enough, the Methow River no longer freezes thickly enough for its ice to be harvested, even if Stanley were to decide to take his old tongs and ice saw out of retirement.)

In 1984 an icebox is only a useless antique, a curious relic which electricity displaced on the Methow in the late 1920's. Was the gain in convenience worth the social loss of the harvest work? Stanley Darwood does not think so.

52

When I started out here in 1921 we had a lot of ice cutting. It was an easy place to get to the river and the ice would thicken here, as much as eighteen inches thick if we had a long freeze, because in that broad bend the water wasn't running at such a speed. Everybody in the neighborhood looked forward to that ice harvest. We all enjoyed working together and seeing a guy fall in and helping drag him out. Heh, heh, heh, heh. I never did fall in. Of course, the river never was more than three or four feet deep since it's so wide there.

The ice harvest always seemed to be around New Year's. But we didn't have long to do it in because the weather would warm up a little and high water would come and run over the top of the ice until it could melt out enough to make an open channel again. So we'd start in when the ice was about a foot thick.

We cut out the ice with a regular ice saw, a thick steel, heavy saw. Its handle had a crossbar so you could take both hands and saw away. You'd cut your blocks about two feet square and they'd be floating around in the water. You had to be careful fishing 'em out with your ice tongs. Then it was just a matter of dragging 'em to wherever your sled was and loading 'em up.

They were heavy. You get into the foot thickness or fourteen inches and they was quite heavy. Anyway, we'd haul 'em to whatever building they had. It didn't have to be a particular type building, just so it would hold sawdust. And you stack 'em up in the middle of the building and leave about a foot of space around each side. And you use snow to pack in between the blocks of ice, so it made a solid block. Then the sawdust goes into that space you leave between the wall and the stack of ice and on top. We used at least a foot of sawdust. Some used eighteen inches. Each person knew how much ice he needed to last from one year to the next. Each family would figure on putting up enough to last until the next year's harvest. And they had iceboxes, you see, to use it in, not refrigerators, since they didn't have electricity.

It was fun. There'd be as many as six or eight people down there all cutting at the same time, more or less helping each other. We'd cut and

cut and fill your sled, and the next guy'd fill the other guy's sled, and so on, see, heh, heh. They was just all helping each other. Naturally, we'd plan on a little party afterwards if there was a way of doing it at all. You betcha! Mostly a kind of get-together with a jug of some kind. It had to be moonshine then.

Oh, we had parties in those days. The house party was the most entertainment there was. You give it this week. I'll give it next week, and so on, up and down the valley. Everybody that could play an instrument at all would play, and everybody would dance and sing and have a great time.

Everybody had their teams and sleds, hansom cutters. Up-to-date things. Heh, heh. Of course, they used to have teams especially for travelling. And we used sleigh bells on the horses so that when they was running along, well, tingle, dingle, dingle, ding-a-ling. Heh, heh, heh, heh. It was lots of fun. The highway wasn't maintained but people used to get out in the wintertime and just go sleigh riding. Bundle up with a few blankets around you and set in that little ol' sleigh and ride up and down the river just for the enjoyment of it.

It ended because new people were moving into the valley who weren't acquainted with that, and it just didn't seem to be the custom any longer. After they quit giving those weekend parties, me and my wife quit running around. But it was a good way because people got together and everybody knew everybody. We didn't have to go to the pool hall or some place like that to get together and celebrate a little bit. No, it was better. That's why they call 'em the good old days. Heh, heh. I can't say it was any worse. Everybody was working and enjoying themselves. We had a good living, so what else did we need?

Eva Beebee

Frontier Bride

During the summer of 1914 a young office secretary from St. Paul, Minnesota, was out west visiting her parents' new homestead on the North Fork of the Flathead. She encountered a handsome fellow named Chauncey Beebee, soon to be one of the first rangers in adjoining Glacier National Park. Their summer courtship, autumn wedding, and new life in frontier Montana give many examples of the meaning of sharing.

Homesteader Chauncey must have seemed a dashing figure for a girl from back East. Not only did he provide fine horses for her daily rides—no small thing in an area which even today has no paved roads—but he was part of the Western color of this outpost of backwoods living. Chance, or Mr. Beebee, as Eva called him, had arrived in the country himself in his parents' covered wagon. He had been born in Iowa. From there his parents had tried homesteading near Edmonton but had been starved out by the severe Albertan winters. So they and another family crossed the Rockies in two covered wagons, looking for better opportunities. The tracks of such immigrant wagons can still be seen on the east shore of Flathead Lake, along with a cemetery beyond which Chance's mother and younger brother never travelled.

Sharing in American experience has not been an empty or aesthetic

56

gesture but a necessary part of survival. A special mix of independence and community ties mark the American character. Without this mix, the surprising accomplishment of people like the Beebees in quickly settling a vast continent would have been impossible.

Chance attended school in Kalispell, northwestern Montana's largest town. When he was eighteen, he and his friend Charlie Wise got a job on the North Fork tending horses for an old Pony Express veteran they called Uncle Jeff. The boys liked the country and homesteaded there in 1908.

U ncle Jeff had a bunch of horses up on the North Fork. Chance and Charlie Wise went up there one winter, just like young eighteen-year-old boys do, to live with the old fella and help feed the horses. They wanted to trap and run around the woods, and he let them live with him. Uncle Jeff was a great big, tall, bony fella with white whiskers down to his waist. If you met him, you'd say, ''Well, there's old Father Time in person.''

Uncle Jeff had told Chance that while riding the Pony Express in St. Joe, Missouri, his legs were so bloody that his pants stuck to them. Chance said that his legs were all calluses on the inside.

After that, Uncle Jeff came into the country up to Fort Benton. When the steamboats quit running there in 1887, why, he and some of the other fellas stayed and stole horses. They had some geese instead of regular watchdogs. Uncle Jeff said that if anyone came around, those geese would make such a fuss! Well, they stole so many horses that Phillips and all those big ranchers over there banded together and took out after them. This old Uncle Jeff was one of the three that outrode the posse. Chance said he never saw a horse that man couldn't ride! Finally the posse gave up when they got into the mountains because they were afraid the horse thieves could hide there and shoot at 'em. So Uncle Jeff was chased off the prairie and into the North Fork.

He was a wicked man. He had steel blue eyes and when he looked at you he'd just pierce you. He told Mr. Beebee that in the early days he and the cowboys over there had nice pinto ponies which they'd take up

to some old Indian's tepee, and they'd trade them for a young squaw. Well, they'd keep her for a year, or until she got pregnant or they got tired of her, and they'd go back to the Indian and make him take her back and give them the ponies again. Then on to another tepee and trade for another squaw.

Uncle Jeff stayed up the North Fork as long as he could until they let him into the Veterans Home because he had been a scout for General Miles. He died and was buried there about 1929.

In 1914, when I came to visit the North Fork, oh, there were just people everywhere. Homestead cabins all through the woods. People from all walks of life. I met Mr. Beebee. He had a bunch of horses and used to take some of us riding every day. I thought the country was so pretty that I stayed.

Everybody was nice and friendly. They'd help each other. Nobody locked their cabins, in case people needed to get in. They always left some split wood and some food for anybody who came along.

Men would go out and work for the Forest Service in the summer to get a grubstake for the winter. Enough for canned goods and flour for sourdough. They trapped in winter. Chance, Charlie Wise, and Hooley Stein had deer meat the year 'round. There were no game laws then. They'd kill a deer when they needed it to eat. When I was married, there was a bounty on bears and lions.

While we rode out to be married in Columbia Falls, my mother and Mrs. Adair and a few other women got a big party set up at Bill Adair's new log store with jack-o'-lanterns on the lawn and everything. When we got back, Charlie Wise set off a shot of dynamite as a signal, and everybody came to dance. There were one hundred and fifty at our wedding. Mrs. Edie Brewster's mother played the organ, and we danced all night to The Missouri Waltz. They didn't think of going home till morning, you know, on account of the bears and everything. There was a dinner out on the lawn and breakfast in the house in the morning.

We were really roughing it in the park from 1917 to 1920. But the tourists in those days were the wealthy people—the Vanderbilts, and the Roosevelts, and the Astors and all, from the East. They used to come in their private railroad cars and then take buses up through the park to the hotels. It was a rich man's playground when we were there.

Chance was experienced with fighting fire. See, in the early days they hired the rangers for their experience. Handling fires and things like that. They were hired as rangers because they were woodsmen. Today they learn it out of books.

At the ranger station we dipped our water out of a crick or a lake and washed our clothes on a washboard. We read by coal oil lamps.

It was pretty lonesome being the only woman. But you know that flu epidemic which was on in 1918? We were never sick a day because of our isolation.

And the game! Oh, there was game. And the bears were thick. You could look out the ranger station window anytime and see two or three bears prowling around your yard. When we did our laundry we'd have to guard it or they'd slap it with their paws and tear it to shreds. So we used to get two big tin lids and bang 'em together till our clothes were dry.

Well, funny things used to happen up the North Fork. Like the story of Hooley Stein's Malone pants.

Hooley Stein got a pension from the government because he'd been in the Spanish War. And so he had more money than the rest of them. Once he bought a nice pair of heavy wool Malone pants and hung them up on the wall and went away for the summer. Charlie Wise came by and saw this nice pair of new Malone pants on the wall. "Well," he thought, "I guess I'll go out to town in a week or so." He didn't have any scissors, but he took the butcher knife and cut off the bottoms to fit him. You see, Hooley was the tallest of the friends and when Charlie tried them on they were too long. When he came back from town he hung them up on the wall again. Later Chance came along and saw that nice new pair of Malone pants and he thought, "Gosh, I'm going out to town in a few days." So he took the butcher knife and he cut them off to suit him, too. His legs were even shorter than Charlie's.

So when Hooley got home those pants were about up to his knees. But that's the way people were. It was all right with Hooley. He'd just put 'em on and wear 'em.

Clara Fewkes

Barn Raisings and Harvesting Bees

Clara Fewkes is a retired schoolteacher who lives in the relocated town of Rexford beside the new Libby Dam reservoir in northwest Montana. Her husband Bill's old general store was moved to nearby Eureka to be the centerpiece of the Tobacco Valley Historical Village. His mercantile's transformation from a working business into a tourist prop is symbolic of the area's overall trend.

People are better off financially today, but I don't think they have as much fun as we did.

And children didn't have as many things before, but they weren't so spoiled. They were more concerned with the rights of others. There was no such thing as vandalism them. Not a bit. You could leave your door unlocked.

Walt Ritter of Trego told me that his family moved into Eureka one winter about 1890 to send him to school. But they left their house open up above Trego, right on the main Fort Steele trail. They never locked their door. They left the woodbox full. They left some food in the cupboard, and dishes and whatever any traveler might need, even a trusty old gun on the wall and a box of shells. They left a note asking whoever might come along to please wind the eight-day clock when it was running down. And would they please refill the woodbox. And if they used the gun, would they please clean it before hanging it back on the wall.

The family was gone about six months, but when they came back home in the spring, the clock was running, the house was clean, the woodbox was full, and the food had been replaced—even more than they had left. Everything was just shipshape.

The country has lost camaraderie, I guess you'd call it. Concern for others. You know, you could get your logs ready and a group of neighbors would come in and you'd have your house up by evening. We used to have lots of barn-raisings and harvesting bees. That kind of neighborliness began to decline when things prospered more, for one thing, and when people moved away and newcomers came in who didn't understand the ways of the West. Especially when the Corps of Engineers built Libby Dam, from '67 to '75, it really shook the community because people scattered. People who would have lived in this relocated Rexford, if they could have, moved somewhere else because they couldn't wait for the Corps to decide what to do about the town. That was one bad thing about the dam because the old Rexford was a wonderful little town. All sorts of things had been done there just by the whole community working together.

For instance, there were a number of fires where there was no fire insurance, and the neighbors helped to build new houses and maybe have a shower for them, and they'd end up with just as much or more than they had in the first place. It was just a case of sharing among one big family. After the Doble house burned, the neighbors went over and got the new house up for them. It wasn't completely finished, but they could move in and work on the inside later.

Helping your neighbors was a way of life then. It was a good way. I remember dropping my own work one morning because I heard that the thrashers had come unexpectedly to my neighbor's house and she was all alone with no one to help her prepare the men's dinner. Of course, a thrashing crew used to be a pretty good bunch of men.

So I just stacked my dishes in the dishpan and took off down the road. I only had a mile to go. And when I walked in there, why, "Oh," she said, "I'm so glad to have help. I didn't know anybody would come and help me." She'd been pretty blue because she didn't see how she could do everything. But I hadn't been there ten minutes when Mrs. Soumi, from the other direction, came and joined us. So there were three of us to get that meal on the table.

Oh, Rexford had its arguments and everything like that, but basically, everyone looked out for each other's interests. Now in the the relocated town there are a lot of people who are not familiar with that kind of life. It's become a retirement area here because there's very little employment left. Well, I remember when the Tuxills first moved in. He'd been an electrical engineer with Detroit Edison back in Michigan, and first he'd retired in Florida and didn't like it. Finally he wound up in Rexford, where he ran a little service station. They were rather proud people. Nice people, but they were from the East. Their service station customers would ask a lot of personal questions, which they resented. "Well, what business is it of theirs, intruding on us that way?" they'd complain. So I told them that they were in a small town where it's like a big family.

Well, neither one of 'em's health was very good, but Tuxill in particular had a heart condition and an ulcer or two. One day he went out to the pumps to fill up a gas tank, and he just collapsed with a bleeding ulcer. That was in the days before we had ambulances. But pretty quick a doctor was called and a car showed up. The neighbors took over and got him to the hospital.

Eventually he recovered and got back and settled down. I was visiting one time and he asked me, "Why in the world would people help out like that?" He was amazed at how something which could have been very serious was handled. I said, Remember me telling you about this "big family" thing? That's the way these people are. If they ask you a personal question, it's not because they're being nosey but because they're genuinely concerned. If something happens and they can help, why, they will. Well, from then on the Tuxills had a whole different outlook on that kind of life.

Joe Yocum

Logging with a Swedish Fiddle

Wiry-looking Joe Yocum is likely to greet a visitor to his banjo-making workshop with a clangy rendition of "Whistlin' Rufus" or some other old tune. But until recently, instead of the banjo his daily instrument had been the "Swedish fiddle" played for piecework—so much money for every thousand feet of timber cut and bucked into log lengths. A sawyer since the late 1920's, Joe still looks the part in his work shirt, suspenders, and logger pants. The only difference is that now he doesn't need to chop the bottoms off his trouser legs.

When you work in the woods it's a lot safer if you cut the hem off, 'cause that's a good way to get hurt if you don't. I knew a guy who got his leg broke when he had it hung up over a limb and couldn't pull loose. His pants wouldn't tear because he had a hem in 'em. A log rolled up and broke his leg. So cut 'em off but not so high the sawdust will get in your boot tops.

Until chain saws came out in 1946 we cut timber with a two-man misery whip, a "Swedish fiddle." It was pretty hard to find a good partner. Somebody might be real good with another guy but not able to work with you. It made quite a difference to have a good partner.

They had two-man power saws when they first come out. Awful heavy. One hundred pounds on the motor end. Well, the tree would hold the saw up as soon as you got started. But packing 'em, that was the thing. Getting it from one tree to another and up and down the logs. That was something else. And on steep ground—then you was working! Oh, it's still hard work, though, with the new saws. Two men in the old days couldn't cut what on the average one does now.

But it's about as dangerous as any job can get. Especially learning, you gotta be pretty careful. It takes about three years, at least, to learn to be a log cutter. Sometimes a tree will fall into another tree, and a limb'll come back and hit you. That's one thing.

And if you don't cut it right, the tree butt can come back over and get you sometimes. I've known quite a few guys got killed and legs broke and one thing or another that way. Once I had a limb come back and hit me and broke a bunch of ribs and punctured a lung. Yeah, I was laid up for quite a while.

You've got to make the right kind of an undercut. That's the cut you fall your tree by. And saw the backcut so the tree won't split. If it splits and leaves a big slab standing up, that's what loggers call a "barber chair." They got a name for everything, loggers have. A "Molly Hogan", that's a knot you tie in a cable. And a "school marm", that's a tree that forks. And if a tree is burnt in, you know, with black spots on it, that's a "cat face." Oh, there's hundreds of 'em. Some of 'em ain't very nice.

You gotta learn how to put in a good undercut so you can fall your tree without a lot of binds and breakage. The undercut's on the side where the tree falls, in the direction the tree will fall. And you've got to cut a level stump without getting all crooked. There's three types of undercut, see, but the idea is always to make a smooth stump. What you call a "Humboldt" undercut is when you saw the vee out from the bottom up. And then another one's just the opposite, when you saw it down. And when they had the big saws they used to just saw two straight notches in, and then you'd have to take an axe and knock out in between. It was just a square cut into the tree. They want a smooth stump with the undercut

on the stump to save wood.

And if you don't cut the backcut correctly, too, your tree'll still barber-chair. To make the backcut you corner the tree up. Cut clear all the way around there, a little at a time, the depth of your bar so your chain'll stay tracked. There's too much chance for a barber chair if you cut straight in.

Watch your backcut to tell when the tree is ready to fall. It'll start opening up. If it don't start opening up when you're up pretty close, you better get a wedge in it. Once it starts opening up, you get out of the road! But don't run straight back. Run off at an angle.

Ninety-nine out of a hundred will go right where you want 'em, once you learn how to fall timber. Yeah, you can drive a stake with 'em. I did it myself, just to see if I could. And lots of times if there's two trees close together, you've got to fall 'em between those two trees. That happens every day, of course. Or say you just want to miss a stump, 'cause it would break the timber. Yeah, beginners, they have their problems for awhile.

Lots of young fellas want to learn today, 'cause it's good money. But they've about got to work with somebody to start with. You're pretty apt to get hurt, or not make any money, or break your saw, one of the three, if you don't.

The first thing for a fella to learn is not to cut himself with the saw. Quite a few new cutters will do that. It makes a bad cut 'cause it tears the meat out that wide. Then you've got nothing left there. And you'll be a long time getting well.

Francis Lufkin

Smokejumper

❖

Sixty-seven-year-old smokejumping pioneer Francis Lufkin of Winthrop, Washington, says that smokejumping "is merely a method of transportation— just the same as breaking in a bunch of people to drive pickups to a fire." Anyone who believes that over-modest analysis has not looked at Lufkin's 1939 first-jump photo of himself complete with two parachutes, heavy logging boots, padded suit, leg bag containing a one-hundred-foot letdown rope, and a football helmet with a wire-mesh face mask.

Firefighting is full of dangers such as falling snags and rolling debris. Many of smokejumping's early experimenters were killed in plane crashes, though there have been very few deaths during actual jumps. Part of the profession's excellent safety record is certainly due to Francis Lufkin's lifelong emphasis on skill and training.

In 1972 Lufkin retired from the U.S. Forest Service as manager of the Winthrop smokejumper base, the place where it all began. At 67 he still has the open, confident look which smiles out to us from that 1939 photograph. From his days as a teenager trapping in the nearby Pasayten Wilderness until his retirement years as mayor of Winthrop he has never liked idleness. Work keeps him young and ready to jump into anything.

This Pasayten Wilderness was known for big forest fires. My first big one was in 1930. Back then a crew going into that country had to walk a day, a day and a half, sometimes all night. It wasn't so tough for me because I was young and I could wear out crews pretty easily. Wear 'em out getting to the fires on the Pasayten River, the Bunker Hill country, and Monument 83 and Trout Creek.

Because it took a long time to get back in there, the Forest Service was looking for a way to get on those fires quicker and prevent such big burns. David Godwin, the man who was looking into it, was the chief of the division of fire control in Washington State. They'd already experimented with dropping tools free-fall or with small parachutes, but about all that did was to break up the tools. About then the Russian military had just engaged in some mass parachute jumps. So David Godwin sent for some of their literature and had it translated. He saw the possibility to apply it here in wilderness areas to fight fire. So he contacted the Eagle Parachute Company back East and a professional parachute jumper named Frank Dary in Los Angeles. He got them together and got a contract up.

They decided the first thing they had to do was build some more strength into the parachutes. Finally in October, 1939, they moved an airplane in here and some professional jumpers. They dropped cargo chutes first with sandbags on them into the timber. Those chutes didn't tear up too bad so they started jumping these men into open areas—for example, right here in back of Winthrop—and then in high meadows, and finally into the timber. Even before they finished they realized it could be done successfully because those parachutes just grabbed onto a tree and held right on.

I worked on that contract all fall. I was just a ground pounder them, chasing fires afoot, operating out of a guard station. I had a pretty good reputation getting to fires on the ground and fighting them.

One day at the end of that contract they just got me into an airplane and I went up and jumped. That was the first time that I'd ever ridden in an airplane, but I'd worked with the fellas all fall and was watching it

pretty close because I thought if there was any opportunity there, why, I'd be interested in it.

At that time my salary was up in the top for ground people other than district rangers, about $135 a month. And we found out that this was going to pay $191 a month. At the tail end of the Depression fifty dollars more was a lot of money to me. I was just beginning to raise a family, so I was glad to get this work.

Well, it was a long step out of that airplane, I'll guarantee you that. But it really didn't bother me much. The airplane scared me more than anything. Just the way it moved in the air in downdrafts and updrafts. Besides that, that particular day it had been raining and I jumped right among the clouds.

The next spring four of us here formed a team. Two were professional jumpers and two Forest Service people, so we could learn from each other. We actually started out with five, but one of the fellas got hurt the first thing falling out of a tree. Methods of getting out of trees and such as that— we just had to develop our own methods.

Also, that same summer the military watched some of our training. That's when the paratroopers came into being. They went immediately to static lines. The following year we did, too, because the hazard of getting everybody to pull his own ripcord was making these professional jumpers kinda grayheaded. They didn't know whether people would pull or not.

When smokejumping came along, why, it was just purty hard for the old-time rangers, dyed-in-the-wool horsemen, to swallow. And they looked out of the corner of their eye at you because anybody who'd do anything like that was crazy. We had quite a job selling smokejumping because they used to think we were nuts.

The smokejumper carries only one piece of equipment, the one-hundred-foot jump rope to descend a tree with. Everything else is dropped to him by parachute—his firefighting tools, his bed, food, chainsaw, gasoline, and water.

Sometimes we can jump within a hundred yards or so of a fire. Other times we keep back a quarter of a mile or so. It just depends on how hard it's burning. Sometimes on smaller fires we can actually use the smoke of the fire as a target. But on the larger fires we usually try to get off on a safe side.

Once he's landed he rolls all his parachute equipment up and puts it in a safe place. And gets his fire pack and takes off for the fire.

Firefighters used to do all the chopping and cutting of logs with a crosscut saw or an axe and all the digging with a grubhoe and a pulaski. We still use those, but now we have chainsaws to cut right-of-ways and helicopters to get you in and out. We've had smokejumpers jump onto two or three fires in one day when we had helicopters to take a ground crew in and the jumpers out.

Don't let me forget to tell you about the heat. When you get on the sunny side of a hill, ground temperature where you are chopping or digging is from five to twenty degrees hotter than the air temperature at chest level. So when you are down against the ground and have the fire temperature, too, why, she really gets hot. That sure wrings you out. And then when you've contained the fire and are mopping it up, why, then you're apt to burn your boots or feet from walking through it.

We try to teach good judgment, but the job can be as dangerous as you make it. On one fire over in Montana we had about fifteen jumpers killed from running through the fire and smoke. Lung damage killed 'em, sucking that hot gas in when they stampeded and ran and ran. The fellas that lay down and dug a coupla little holes, they got two or three black spots on their shirts, but other than that they came out fine. But the others just stampeded.

There's always the chance the fire will get out of control, get away from the jumpers. But normally they can do hot spot work and flank it. As they pick up the hot spots they gradually build a line all the way around the fire. Then once they think they've controlled its spread they start mopping up—chopping the fire out of logs or lifting them up in the air to let them cool off or smearing the fire with dirt.

After the fire if the jumper can't get a helicopter or pack string ride, then he's got to backpack at least a hundred pounds, often over terrifi-

74

cally rough country. Often it's so steep he lets his gear roll down the mountain and picks his way down after it.

For years we'd been training for a big fire bust, and finally in 1970, why, it happened. We had over two hundred fifty jumpers from all of the other bases and all kinds of trained ground crews from all over the United States. During that one week we fed better that five thousand meals to fire fighters who were passing through. At our airport for three days straight we had more air traffic than Spokane International. We just put the smoke-jumpers here and there on the fire to pick up some hot spots which were way out ahead of the regular fire crews. Usually a helicopter would pick 'em out of there to come back and get suited up to be ready to fly out to another one. That season we made about 1250 jumps on around 250 different fires.

A smokejumper can make five to six thousand dollars a summer—if he hangs on to it. The only requirement outside of age and physical condition is at least one summer's experience fighting fire. Then the parachute jumping is merely a method of transportation. During the spring a new rookie jumper is given 168 hours of very concentrated training. Much of it is physical, including the method of getting out of trees, which through the years has been developed to where these fellas can get down in less than a minute.

I guess it's dramatic to some people, but to the firefighter, a guy that's been in the business, it's just lots of dirty work, plain hard labor that takes all the sap out of you. The main job is to go put the fire out and do it safely and get back safely.

Clyde Smith

Logging Horses

Like his late father and brother, 65-year-old Clyde Smith is an old-time unreconstructed horse logger. Although he had logged during the '60's and '70's with huge "cats" and skidders, he was never happy with the steel, diesel oil, and smoke. Finally in the late '70's he took up the reins of Percherons and Belgians once again.

After beginning with his father at the age of twelve, Clyde had horse-logged until 1959, fully twenty years after most people had abandoned it. In 1978 I encountered him fire-salvage clearcutting a very steep hillside in the watershed of Troy, Montana. He was glowingly happy to be behind the lines and chains of Sam and Ben. Aluminum hard hat set at a jaunty angle, he easily strode up the steep slopes of his world of skid roads and low stumps. "They don't want no machines up here at all," he said enthusiastically, "so all we got are power saws and a truck to load and haul with. That ground's so loose that a cat might climb it, but a skidder couldn't."

Doug Smith, a thinner, less husky man than his father, hitched the team to a freshly cut sixteen-foot log and was about to skid it down the hill to the landing where his truck's mechanical arm would load it for the trip to the sawmill. The harnesses and chains creaked and groaned and the horses tugged and snorted. They quickly gained momentum and thundered down the skid road.

"Horse logging today don't take near the manpower," said Clyde, "because we've got power saws for that swamping. And then, of course, loading, too. We loaded with the horses then, see. There was no power at all. We didn't have no dozers, nothin'. We started in the wintertime and had to work every day, otherwise with the snow we'd have to quit. We worked seven days a week when it was snowing. But now we've got better tools. We don't have any better axes and stuff like that, though. That part is hard to get. Like peaveys and cant hooks. There's no blacksmith to set 'em up. I just happen to have some my dad had."

Clyde showed me the twenty-foot-long skid chains which trailed behind the horses' complex, heavy leather harnesses. Also, he pointed out "dogs," iron-spiked connectors used in towing several logs at a time and designed to prevent heavier, faster ones from dangerous tobogganing on steep descents. I picked up a dog variation called a "J-grab," an anchor-shaped affair with a ring for attaching lines. Clyde said it was useful in self-releasing a heavy string of runaway logs. "We dog the logs together just like a string of wieners, drive the J-grab into the back log, put the horse rigging astraddle it, and hook into its ring. If the logs start to go, they'll just run right out from under them and slide down the hill. I've seen logs that would go two hundred feet before they stopped."

If you don't know what you're doing and don't get everything lined up right, you're gonna cripple horses and kill somebody. It's skill! Half of this is skill."

Doug returned with the team to swing a long tree trunk out of the skidway. While the skid chains clanked and the horses snuffled, Clyde's chainsaw whined into green limbs. Doug backed the horses up to the butt end so that he could attach his skid chains. "Back, Ben. Back," he yelled. "Easy, Sam. Ho!" When he had it just right he urged his animals to take up the slack. "Little bit, fellas. Little bit," he cried. They obediently moved forward slightly until everything was ready and he started them moving his new log. "Easy now. Careful." The tree moved with a weighty crunching of branches.

I worked with some of those fellas like Preach Fields who set choker. Boy, it took a pretty good man and they were all heavyset. They had to have lots of muscle 'cause them chokers, you might be carrying a hundred and fifty pounds or maybe more.

Everyone had a lot of pride in their work. These fellas I worked with were the true lumberjacks. You'd never see a swamper pick up a set of lines. Everyone had a specialty. A jammer. A sawyer. A swamper. A skinner. A cant hook man. You give a cant hook man a peavey and he'd wrap it around your neck because they didn't like that spike which could stick in the ground and likely break their leg.

When we started a job like, say, a couple hundred million feet in a basin, we'd go in there and build a camp out of logs. Build a good barn and a good cookhouse. We'd always have a good cook 'cause where the good food was you'd find the best lumberjacks. The Diamond usually had them, too.

Anything you could mention—they had it. Fresh fish in season. The finest bacons and hams and beef. They usually had a tote road into camp and they'd bring that stuff in on a pack horse. Oh, and canned or fresh vegetables. I've been in a camp where they had every kind of meat and fish. And for breakfast, it was just like a banquet. Bacon and eggs and hotcakes and French toast and strong black coffee which could float a wedge. Bacon and ham and link sausage all for one meal. And hotcakes! They'd eat a stack that high. I seen my brother eat seventeen one morning. He was just a kid, a wild man working hard. That's the way they ate. I seen some of them guys like chute builders, short, heavyset Finns, who'd work like horses. They'd take a whole platter of wieners and scrape 'em right off on their plate. Why, you couldn't believe it. And they'd go out and pack logs around like they was a crane or something.

Oh, we had characters all right. Like one they called High Trestle Red. They had handles like that. Whiskey Bill. Moonlight Joe. My older brother, Bud, they called him Mad Ivan. He was a big brute, a typical lumberjack. He made money and he spent it like water. He's dead now, but he was his own worst enemy. He grew up with the old jacks like I did. He was a speedball. He'd have had this job done and been looking for more. Well, I would have then, too. I could have skidded this whole thing in half the time we're taking.

My father died in '61, but most of his logging he done with horses. He always kept horses, right up until the end. He liked it and it was cheap. He could produce a log cheaper'n anybody. He had more money in his pocket than the guys with fancy equipment like me. I had thirty to forty thousand dollars worth of equipment and, boy, by the time I paid all my bills I was just making a living just like he was. And I had to get up at four o'clock in the morning and drive for a hundred miles and then run like a madman for eight hours and come a hundred miles back home. I done that year in and year out. Or stay in camp like where I was up the Thompson River for four years and just come home weekends. And we'd skid as high as a hundred thousand a day with one cat. Big stuff. Those machines would come in to the landing with as much as five thousand feet at a time. But we was just making a living.

Pretty near all them old-timers like my dad were conservative fellas. They'd say, "Don't buy anything on time. That money goes to New York. Keep your money at home." And they were right! That way the country would be in a lot better shape.

So horse logging is that much cheaper. It's coming back. These guys spend a fortune on equipment to go out after second growth. On little stuff they can't even get enough volume to pay for their fuel. At the end of the year I'll have more money than they do for the amount that I've invested. You check them loggers. There ain't one out of ten that's making it pay. If your skidder costs forty thousand dollars, you've got to have big trees to get the volume. I'm an expert on that because I skidded as much as any man. I had a D4D, one of the late models. A big cat tears up so much ground that the only place where they can get away with that now is on private land. And on clearcuts they compact the ground so much that the roots of planted trees won't penetrate.

And you get more laughs out of these horses! Like one day I was away to pick up some stuff and Doug, he forgot to feed the horses their oats.

Well, that's a crime in my book. And theirs, too. They let him know! Old Sam, he was so mad he pawed and he looked at Doug. Well, Doug figured out what was the matter and he got to laughing. That horse was trying to tell him that he should have given him some oats. I said, "Don't take him out no more if you can't remember that. Not my horses. That's all they get outta life, that feed, and they're entitled to it 'cause they earn it." Of course, Doug didn't do it intentionally.

The horses don't mind the work. In fact, we used to have horses that'd come right back up to the swamper without no driver. I've had a lot of fellas tell me about one horse. They'd hook him onto a log and he'd go to the landing and go back and forth half a day at a time. We had an old brown horse my dad brought from Oregon, and he done that. My dad was loading cars and old Lad was across the railroad track. They had two skids, see, going up onto the car to send the log up. And you'd have a chain around the middle. Just one line. And it took a man on each end. So the old horse was over on the other side of the car pulling and they couldn't even see him. He'd go and stop when my dad would holler. Nobody else could drive him. If somebody else tried to drive old Lad, he'd open his mouth and take right after them. But my dad would say, "Whoa, Lad," and he'd stop. Back, gee, or turn around and come back. He'd just make that circle and they'd load the whole car and never drive him.

Ben and Sam are a good pair of horses for that long line skinning, when you turn 'em loose and drive 'em without the lines. But I told Doug this morning that he's gonna have to start driving 'em 'cause they could pull five logs, but they've got so they won't stop if they've got three attached to take to the landing. The roan, he knows right where to park it. So they run down and then they get to rest ten minutes before the skinner gets there.

So they don't mind working—if you take care of them and don't abuse them. I've told people when I work my horses they put on weight, not lose it. That's the one thing that we had trouble with in the old days. Too many people abused their horses. They didn't know when to quit. They was money-hungry, greedy. My brother was one of them. When he got in the woods he was a wild man. He'd run right over the logs. He'd skid

81

and load sixteen thousand feet a day. Big timber logs. And he done that day after day. He might put in ten hours. Them horses would hoist them onto the truck. That's work for two teams. Sixteen thousand! It was good timber but it was big, heavy hemlock. He'd skid them in and load four loads every day.

When we'd get around one another I'd take the lines. I couldn't stand it. I said if I'm gonna be around, I'll drive 'em. Otherwise we're gonna get in a fight.

He had a beautiful team of horses and they were scared to death of him. He'd pull down on them and they'd dig holes right in the solid rock. I seen 'em throw ice over their heads. We were loading poles, big eighty-foot class poles that went to Minneapolis. They were four feet in diameter on the big end. And green. We put eleven of them on a regular truck and blew every tire on it. We had to stop and unload them. We didn't know they were near that heavy. He was loading uphill and had ice shoes on them and they were throwing ice, rock, and stuff over his head. And he loaded them eighty-foot poles and set 'em right on the truck. Oh, his horses never lost weight, but he mauled 'em around somethin' fierce.

Of course, most all the horses we had in the old days was just out of cayuse mares and big stallions. The average horse then weighed about fifteen hundred. You didn't see many big horses. They'd play out on steep ground like this. But this team is a good pair, about the size we used in the old days when we were logging steady.

The roan is all Percheron but the bay is half draft, half bow and arrow. Anything with spots on it they can register as an Appaloosa. Chief Joseph had them spotted horses. They've been around a long time. Very smart. But his legs are lighter bone and will give out before the other one's.

Them horses there will come in with fifteen hundred feet at a time. Five big trees. They run down the hill with 'em. The roan goes to one side or the other to speed it up because the faster it moves the easier it is to pull.

A chunk came loose up there and Doug hollered, ''Look out!'' I run one way and them horses, they jumped from here to that tree. Boom, they were gone, just like lightning. They were watching that and jumped clear

82

of the skid road. I got open bridles, see, so they can watch behind them. You ain't gonna catch them unless you get them fouled up behind a stump or somethin'.

I like Percherons best because they're so smart and easy to handle. I've got Belgians, too, but they're so stubborn that they'll just walk up and stomp right on your foot. Percherons are easier to train. I can talk to them and they'll get around over them logs, stop, or do anything I want 'em to do except quit eating.

They'll get out there and they can find more stuff, fireweed, just like elk or deer. Like when I took them up selective logging in the park for seven months where two hundred fifty thousand trees blew down at the Indian Creek campground. I couldn't get anybody to go so I sawed it and I swamped it all myself. I wish you could have seen that when I got through. Places I logged in winter where I left no scar at all. All you can see are the stumps. I'd skid them out of the little trees before turning 'em and then cut them into short logs. Quite a job!

Doug has just started and, oh, I get after him once in awhile. In fact, I get a little rough. I get aggravated sometimes the way he handles the lines. He might have a horse turned clear around here and he'll forget to let up on the line. And anything that hurts them horses gets me.

What we need is a good sawyer. Doug is just learning. I'm no sawyer. I never did saw. It takes a real man to saw and get speed up. One of them guys'd lay this whole dang thing down in a week. If we hired a first-class sawyer, we'd double our production every day. So far we haven't had enough manpower to keep this one team busy. They can skid more logs than we can cut, swamp, load, and haul.

What we eventually want to do is operate about three teams. Doug would run the landing and load the truck. With the horsepower we have now, and with about six men, we could take a job, say a million feet, and do it in three months. And as soon as I got enough guys trained I could just relax—taking care of the harnesses and feed, laying out the skid trails, and giving the skinners heck!

It's hard work. There's no easy way. Most guys don't want to work that hard. You can screen maybe a hundred men before you find a man that wants to do that. But I'll tell you, it don't take long to get in good physical shape. Doug there, he'd been trucking and just sitting in the cab. Out here he was groaning for a month and thought he was gonna die. Me, I was the same way. I'd been running cat for the last twenty years. God, I told him if I ever get out of shape again I'm gonna quit work and not try to get back in shape. But I'm not too old yet—as long as I can still stagger around.

Bert Wilke

River Pig

◈

Where does drudgery stop and the pride of work begin? Traditional logging had a wealth of lore which reinforced its workers' self-esteem. For instance, a cant hook man would never touch a peavey, and many sawyers would never let even the camp saw filer gum and file their "Swedish fiddles." The jobs in the woods were just that—jobs—but they often had an extra dimension compounded of risk and comradeship. In the great turn-of-the-century logging camps which dotted the hills of northwest Montana it took a true professional to handle the exacting, often dangerous work of falling, swamping, loading, and moving millions of board feet.

River pigs were among the most colorful of the woodsmen. In the days before logs went to the mills atop huge trucks, they were floated down rivers such as the Kootenai, the Flathead, and the Clearwater. Even creeks which today look too small once supported heroic springtime log drives, thanks to water released from dams in sudden "splashes."

Bert Wilke, of Fortine, Montana, was born in 1893, not quite long enough ago to be classified as an old-timer, according to his way of thinking. "You was an old-timer in the Flathead," he says, "if you was there before the railroad come in." Although he missed that by a couple of years, he was active in several woods specialties in the great era of Northwest ox and horse logging. While he was still in grade school he learned to ride the logs well enough that eventually he participated in the most dangerous drive of them all—Marble Creek.

Our first school here was at the ranger station at Ant Flat [Montana] where my stepdad was the ranger. The next year they built a log schoolhouse over the hill from Trego right on the river bank. Then they started driving there in the spring of 1907. Of course, that was quite a thrill for us kids, and we had to be out on the logs.

When the Baker Brothers had logged off the town of Whitefish and that country they had one of the bigger logging outfits around. A camp crew of from eighty to one hundred men. When they moved up here in 1907 they had two yokes of bulls. Each of the bigger oxen weighed a little over a ton. They used those yokes in the fall for putting in the skidways and for short skidding. The logging in this country was all done in the winter because before the ground froze you could only skid a short distance since the logs would dig in.

The Baker Brothers' camps always had a couple of big bunkhouses, a blacksmith shop, a saw filer's shop, and a wanigan, a store for all the supplies, clothing, shoes, rubbers, and tobacco, stuff the guys'd need. You could even buy blankets or sougans there. At that time, why, all the lumberjacks carried their own beds and those camps'd get fulla bedbugs and lice. Men would pack 'em from one camp to another. You could build a new camp but before a month it would be lousy. You just had to put up with them. A lotta guys would mix powder in with their blankets to keep the bedbugs from keeping 'em awake.

Bunkhouses had double bunks, upper and lower. In the evening the upper ones would be the warmest, but when the fire died away, why, they'd be the coldest. So everybody would want to sleep in a lower bunk.

Beds were hay to spread your blanket on. Most of them old lumberjacks had comforters, what they called sougans, just a cotton-filled square you could buy for two dollars. They were kinda warm at first before the cotton batting would separate. Later you could hold them up and look through 'em.

Money was hard to get in them days and you had to be on the ball. In the early '20's sawyers and swampers got thirty dollars a month and board. The four-horse teamsters got fifty-five dollars a month for driving them. Skidding teamsters got forty-five. The top loader man got seventy-five and board. He had to know his stuff because them sleighs had to be loaded right on what they called the pin so that they would turn. You load ten thousand feet of logs, why, that's a lot of weight on there!

A lot of the crew stayed with Baker Brothers year after year. When men were hard to get, all the Bakers had to do was hire their old cook, George Helders. He was one of the best camp cooks in the country. All they had to do was hire him and all the lumberjacks they wanted would flock to where the best grub was. He was a big, rawboned guy who got along with everybody. But you didn't dare talk around them old camp cooks. They'd shut you up in a hurry. Well, if you got eighty men a-talking. . . you could ask someone to pass something but that was all. Some of them old cooks, they got pretty mean.

But where they really fed good was on the Marble. You couldn't beat it! You had breakfast about six in the morning and then at ten o'clock they'd send a hot lunch out. Oyster soup or clam chowder. Then again at three o'clock they'd send out another warm meal. Evening, why, you come in the camp and had supper. Four meals a day!

My brother and I was working here and we heard them old river pigs telling that the Marble was starting up, what kind of grub they had, and what they was paying. They was paying five dollars a day there and only three here. So we quit here and went up on the Marble.

They paid wages according to the stream. The Marble Creek drive was the most notorious because it took two or three guys every year. When you fell in you never got out, because it was all fast water. Steep banks and no water ahead of them jams when they come down. Just dry crick bed. The water was all behind. Oh, it was a dangerous stream. That's the reason they paid more money.

River pigs were mostly all young guys—around forty years old. Oh, there was some older men that had been at it all their lives but you had to be pretty fast on your feet.

When they first started the drive up there above Trego them river pigs would be out on logs on a Sunday just to be catting around. An old river pig would have a couple of us kids set down on a log and he'd take his pike pole and paddle that log all over the lake. Control it and keep it from turning. They were good. They had to be!

So we kids put a couple of dry tamarack into Murphy Lake here and we'd cuff them logs every Sunday during the summer. We all rigged up caulked shoes and had them on and that's all. Four or five of us would get on one log and we'd burl it till there was just one guy on there. It took a long time to learn to control a log out in the water with your feet. But us kids got so we could stay on the sunny side of a log.

Three of us kids, as soon as we were out of the eighth grade, we started to work on the drives. In the spring the river pigs would flock into this country about the time they figured the drive would start. I've seen it here when we had five or six saloons in Fortine and there'd be a couple of hundred river pigs move in. Them old river pigs, you know, they didn't cotton to us kids. But we'd watch our chance to get out on the same log with 'em and cuff 'em in.

I remember a hell of a nice river pig song about driving logs.

You sit upon the mossy banks,
And watch the logs go by.
They say there is no rear to sack,
For the logs rode high and dry.

When you're on the rear of a drive you pull logs with your pike pole out into the main stream from where they're caught in the brush. You sack the logs in and keep 'em floating. From the upper end you'd clean the stream as you'd go down, working on logs all the time. Generally if you have a good log that holds you up in good shape, why, you kinda stay with that one.

But you couldn't ride a log in Marble Creek. In that country the streams are fast. The banks are so steep that logs at the front end of them jams would just go end over end.

Marble Creek was all summer logging. They had four dams and they had them timed so that the splashes would all come right on the second. That's the way they floated their logs down about five miles from the upper camp. And at the foot of where sluices and chutes came down off the hills logs would build up in what they called jackpots. They kept piling them up with splashes and chutes all summer until the logjam would be about thirty feet high at the lower end and five miles long. That's what the river pigs had to break up when they started driving in the spring.

The Marble was a deep snow country with eighteen feet of snow at the upper camp. In the spring they sent in about sixty men to shovel out the twenty-two miles of trail so they could get the pack stock in to the camps.

Then they had half of the crew shovelling the snow off of the top of the jam and the other half cutting the front end out to place a charge of powder in there. The powder was timed to go off just when their splash hit the upper end of the jam. The powder would loosen up the front end so that when the water hit it would move a bunch of logs.

One day about twenty of us were working on the front end of the jam. The logs were piled up thirty feet high and there was not even enough water to get your feet wet. All of the water was in back and when that force started to move the jam there was nothing to stop it. We was working on that front end when it started to move, but we all got out of there in time.

They had a steam donkey half a mile downstream up on a bench above the crick. That donkey was breaking up a jackpot where the logs had piled up a hundred feet high. We were supposed to let the engineer know when a big jam broke loose so that he could unhook his bull block. That's a big pulley anchored across the crick for the inch-and-a-half cable used in breaking up jackpots. We couldn't notify him but that old donkey engineer knew just what had happened because his old donkey was bouncing up and down where it was anchored onto about a dozen stumps. Now he didn't want to break his cable because they'd packed it up there over those Marble Moun-

tain switchbacks the year before on a string of thirty sets of mules. That was quite a job! They even had swinging bridges to cross the crick with those mules. So he just paid that cable out real slow.

They estimated that there was eight million feet in that one bunch of logs alone. It went twenty miles in a little over an hour to the St. Joe River. They said you could walk across the Joe River on logs that had just come out of Marble Creek. And there was about a hundred thousand feet of logs wound in around that cable. It took us a couple of days to pick them out.

The Marble took guys every year. It took three guys while I was there. One guy, we were working on the jam before the tail end of the splash was out, which we should't have done, and some of the logs shot out. This guy was right out in the middle of the crick, and if he'd have jumped and angled toward shore and kept his feet, the water wasn't too deep, he could probably have stayed on his feet and got out. But he didn't, and he rode down and the last we seen of him he was in between two logs when he went down around the curve. You couldn't keep up with him. They never found nothin' of him.

Fortunately, Bert Wilke made his living primarily with pack animals and not with jackpots and dangerous rivers. He learned the skill from his step-father, who had been a packer at mines in British Columbia until becoming a Forest Service ranger at Kintla Lake in 1901 (in what since 1910 has been Glacier National Park).

He taught me, but for a good packer he was too slow and too particu-lar. He'd take him too long. When I was going good I could load up ten head in about fifteen minutes. You know, I had the loads all cargoed with the decker saddles. Before, when we first started out with them old sawbucks, we had to use the single diamond and the double diamond hitch or the squaw hitch. But when they got the decker saddles, why, you cargoed up your loads for each side pack and you throwed 'em up on the side and put that one hitch on. It just took about a minute to load a mule then since you just put that one hitch. But that's one thing about packing—you don't make any false moves.

I learnt a lot of that from a big old Irishman named Lee Parlin. Every knot, why, when you undone it, it needed just a jerk. Everything, even your pack saddle, your latigos. When you took your pack saddle off, just a jerk and your latigo was loosened up. I used to try to beat him saddling up and unsaddling, but I couldn't. He'd do it so damn easy and smooth. He wouldn't be rushing. He was taking his time, but every move counted.

He and I packed here in '27. If we'd both go, we could move a big trail camp in one trip.

When I first started packing for the Forest Service I tried to hold 'em down to two hundred pounds. But a lot of the camp ration boxes for twenty-five-man outfits weighed around one hundred fifty pounds apiece. That was too much for some of the trails, especially to lookouts. The lookout rations, big boxes of canned goods, weighed one hundred and fifty-two pounds, one on each side. They wouldn't let me split 'em and make lighter loads. When you packed up to a lookout one mule had practically all the weight. And you had to travel according to your heaviest load. No more than a mile and a half an hour on the mountain trails. Whereas if I could split it up and put one hundred fifty or two hundred pounds on each of them, why, I could go right along. But we had some rangers that were the dumbest things I think that ever hit this country. You know, no experience. They learned it all in school and when they'd come out to get the practical part of it, why, they were hard to work for. They just didn't know.

I've been around horses all my life. When I worked in the woods I generally drove teams. I don't know. I's kind of a horse crank, in a way.

But when they got the mules, why, I got along fine with them, too, even though I'd never been around them very much before. I know one spring I had a bunch of young mules that were just halter broke. They were snorty and they'd kick at you. But after supper when they were tied up I'd go around and fool with them. I got so I could catch 'em anyplace. I never tried to rope a horse or a mule, either one, 'cause when you're out in the sticks you gotta be able to walk up to them and catch 'em.

You get a string broke, why, you kinda take a liking to 'em and they take a liking to you, too. I know. In '35 I quit packing. Then in '36 my brother and I, we bought a tie mill up on Jim Creek. A packer from Ant Flat stopped at the camp with my old string. Them old mules spotted me and started braying. I went over and talked to them. That man told me, ''You better keep away from them or you'll get kicked.'' No, they won't kick me, I says. They all know me.

I don't know. You kinda get attached to 'em. You hate like hell to have anybody else monkey with 'em.

Ralph Thayer

Timber Cruiser

Ralph Thayer worked for many years for the U.S. Forest Service, often alone and far out in the wilderness. In winter he cruised timber, that is, he catalogued the tree resources of carefully measured plots of national forest land. Because this work was done on foot and not by air in those days, Frank became an expert maker and repairer of the snowshoes used in timber cruising.

Summertime saw him out in the same mountains blazing stock trails for construction crews to build. Many of those trails were abandoned in recent decades by government cost-cutters with the result that "you can't hardly find them anymore." Pack strings and trails have been replaced with roads and airplanes.

Few government people today would agree to work under the conditions of Ralph Thayer's solitary, primitive employment. After all, expectations were different in those days—especially in the matter of dedication.

W hen you cruise timber you mark out a control line. Say you'd pace out ten chains, that's ten times sixty-six feet, and cruise everything in that. If it was in a draw, you'd have to go right up over the mountain, not around. No matter how steep it was you'd have to go straight. Some places you'd have to hang on with your hands to make it.

It's so rough going straight up over the hills that you'll break the strings of your snowshoes. When I worked as a timber cruiser for the Forest Service I kept their snowshoes in shape.

I learned some of it from Charlie Wise. All the trappers — Charlie Wise, Hooley Stein, and guys up in Canada— had to make their own then. They used moose hide, which makes the best webbing. Or you could use a green cowhide.

Put the hide in a tub with warm water and strong soap to slip the hair. It all depends on the weather how long it will take. Scrape all that hair off with a knife and then cut the hide in strips about six feet long, head to tail lengthwise with the critter. Cut 'em better'n a half inch wide. Tie maybe seven or eight or nine strips together using slits in the ends of each one.

Then take the bark off a couple of trees about ten or fifteen feet apart and wrap your long strip around them trees as tight as you can. Those strips are green and wet, so twist 'em up with a two- to three-foot stick. Twist 'em up till maybe you break one and you have to fix it. Then twist it up again until you've got all the stretch out of the green hide. That way, when you make the snowshoes they won't be baggy.

Along the cricks find willows with the big end maybe twice as big as my thumb. You have to scrape the bark off and soak 'em good. Drive some nails into a board in the shape you want your shoe to be, round or oblong. Then just wind the wet willow right around the nails and leave it set. Where the ends of the willow come together on the board put a staple in there to hold it. Sometimes the wood will crack a little at the bend after a few days, so you've got to pound it a little there to break that sinew.

Mountain ash is the best wood. I used to get mine from a Pennsylvania fella I worked with up in the Canadian oil fields. When he got home he sent me a bundle of mountain ash strips just the right size for my snowshoes.

Then just wrap the strings around the willow frame. You have to start with the piece of webbing your foot's going to be on. Tie it on one side and come across and back in what they call a snowshoe tie. Then you lace it starting at a certain place in order to come out in squares.

Paint 'em with varnish like boughten ones or else the wood will wear out too fast and on a warm day the leather will soak up water and stretch.

Of course, the Indians were the ones who made 'em first.

Old Dad Meyers that lived here years ago before I did, well, he said the Kootenai Indians used to come over the Whitefish Divide and steal horses from the Flatheads and take 'em back. In the next few days or so the Flatheads would go over there and steal 'em all back again and some of theirs. That was before my time.

I relocated that old Yakinikak trail, the trail of the moose. It went up and down so much that it was tough on the horses, so I cut them hills out. I don't know whether I could find the old trail now or not. It's been so long. So much brush grown up in places. It'd be so different.

A fellow by the name of Bosworth that worked for the Forest Service, he and I were in the same outfit in France. I worked for him and we were mapping this north end. We'd keep track of what range and what township we were in and the sections. We turned the dope in to the main office and then they took our map and some other ones and put them together to make a big map.

When I was locating trails I'll bet I'd blaze on the average ten miles a day, every day, Sundays and all. But I had to run a rough preliminary first, five, six, or eight or so miles, from the starting point at the main trail on the river. Climbing all the time. Sometimes I'd have to go over twice to see which way was best. It took a lot of hiking.

Oh, some of the kids that are hiking now are pretty good. You see so many of them hiking miles and miles. But holy smokes, we had it a little rougher since they can get stuff that we couldn't get. Like when I was locating trail, I lived out of a frying pan. I made my own bannock, that's the same as biscuit dough only you put it in a frypan. You mix it up, so much baking powder and salt and flour, and you make it just like biscuit dough so it'll stay when you tip the pan up to catch the heat from the fire. Of course, biscuit dough you don't have to raise, but I used to make fresh bread, too, but I'd let it raise right in the pan.

Before there was a road here I located all these trails from the main river trail. Up pretty near every crick. Alone.

I was raised in the big city and went to school in St. Paul. But here you had to be so you wouldn't get lonesome. You'd go off by yourself and when night came you'd bed down and go to sleep. I just come by it naturally. Some others got homesick and had to leave.

Howard Miller

Steelhead Water

Steelheaders are not ordinary fishermen. They're crazier.

December to March is prime steelhead season, the time when the ocean-going trout temporarily return to their spawning grounds in Northwest rivers and streams. Unlike salmon, which die after spawning, steelhead then swim back to their lives in the sea.

Say the word "steelheader" and most local people will think of freezing rain, icy mists, and bone-chilling winter storms. Steelheaders themselves tell gleeful stories of times when there was so much floating ice that they had a difficult job finding open water for casting.

The Skagit River is to steelheading what the Kentucky Derby is to horseracing. The sport began on the Skagit in the early '30's and some of its elite early-day pioneers like Bud Meyers still fish the river regularly. Once Bud explained to me how modern steelheading with a rod and reel began. "My grandparents homesteaded in Lyman in 1876," he said, "and my aunt was the first white child born there. My dad loved to trout fish with a little trout wheel and one hundred foot of line. Mother, though, never would use a reel in trout fishing. She just had an eight-foot line on a pole. Well, almost a mile up from Lyman, on Jim's Slough, about eighty Indians lived in a longhouse. *When I was eleven I found an Indian dugout canoe in a logjam after a flood. My dad was about the first man to use a rod and reel for steelhead, and he and I steelheaded out of that dugout. I used to pole it standing up like an Indian."*

Bud's friend Howard Miller was an insurance man for thirty-five years until his steelhead hobby and his political interests turned him toward full-time guiding and politicking (an elected position as a county commissioner).

As we drive to a river landing to "empty in," I wonder about the attraction of these dark, icy February mornings. Howard's conversation is a mixture of thinking out loud about the county road's potholes and enthusiastic fish tales. He is 68, has lived in the county all his life, and is more comfortable in the outdoors than behind a desk dealing with government red tape. I trust him completely with our lives on the often treacherous Skagit.

At the landing preparing the boat Howard is as at home as any man can be. Why is he a steelheader? "I like the outdoors," he explains as the flat-bottomed square-ender floats off its trailer. "The birds and ducks and deer and otter and beaver. There's so much to see."

A definite understatement, I learn as we speed noisily upstream past the Hanging Cedar—Howard and his friends have names for everything on the river— looking for some good "holes."

A "hole" is an area of slower, deeper water beside the fast currents, probably less a physical feature of the bottom than an amalgam of tradition and hope. "Holes" are part of steelheading's mystique, like bait and the weather.

I hunch my shoulders against the cold rush of dawn air. Ahead of us, goldeneyes hurriedly take flight while others wing in singly to land astern. Mists rise and shift to reveal and then recurtain the rugged landscape. The dark blue mountains abeam and upstream gleam with snow. Mount Sauk's lookout cabin is a tiny speck above us. Glinting dully on the water, the sun barely shines through the low, gray sky. Even my heavy clothes feel inadequate until the motor stops and we begin to drift.

The silence is very welcome. Jams of mottled driftwood crowd the sandbars. Crossing our bow to a tall alder, one of the river's many wintering bald eagles begins a vigil for dying, spawned-out salmon. And beneath us the

100

bottom's rocks and pebbles are surprisingly visible in water which I always associate with summer's greenly murky glacial melt.

We drift to a new hole along banks thickly lined with cedar and fir. Two great blue herons flap ponderously past and a colorful Steller's jay comes to pick at moss on an alder limb. The morning grows more and more beautiful. Howard's sinker bumps along the bottom about twenty feet away. Imagine drifting, or "boondogging," like this every winter day. These grown men are Huck Finns, but hard-working ones.

A water ouzel flies by and stops to bob on the gravel bar opposite us. His happy, bubbling call pervades the river. Sure, steelhead are delicious to eat, and there is the camaraderie of the men in the boat, and Howard with thirty fish this season is a phenomenal guide. . . my reservations vanish. Maybe I am crazy, too.

T he Skagit is one of the few streams on the West Coast that has all the species of salmon—sockeye, humpback, coho, silver, chum, king—and the steelhead. It's one of the great streams of fishing. In the early days people just didn't bother about the steelhead. They didn't have the time or the equipment, and it wasn't the sport it is now.

This river is a very dangerous river. It looks so beautiful that we have a lot of newcomers and ecologists that just get very poetic about how peaceful and wonderful it is and they don't know what they're doing and we have to go looking for the bodies. Recently a man who had guided on the river for twenty-five years flipped his boat over. It was just a miracle that he lived. This river is an extremely fast river. The size of it fools people, but some of these riffles go eight or ten miles an hour. That amount of water can sink a large boat so fast you wouldn't even realize it. Looking at the water where it's running calm and smooth they think it's very safe out there. But the minute you hit a stationary object you've had it because that water piles right up and comes right in your boat and pulls it under. Years ago they didn't have good boats and people fished from the bank.

That's what the plunkers still do in the lower stretches of the river. They plunk their bait out. They use six to eight ounces of lead, whatever

it takes to hold their lures. They'll throw it out with a heavy sinker where the fish'll be going by and that anchors their bait. If they use a lure instead of bait, they have what we call a wing bobber, a colored piece of balsa wood with little wings on it to make it turn in the water where it's anchored.

The plunkers are usually older people who can't stand the rigors of being out. They'll take a few boards and make a cabin of some kind with a stove made of an old oil drum. They can look out at their pole propped up at the edge of the water with their line out in the current. Sometimes they tie a white rag around the pole, and if that's jerking they know they have a fish. Or a turkey bell. It's like a cowbell, about an inch and a half through.

I think it's great. I seen men out there seventy-five years old that's retired and they can gather in the morning and get their poles set out. They play pinochle or cards and every once in a while they look out to see if their poles are bobbing. Of course, the plunkers don't do as well as we do up here with our drift boats drifting from hole to hole. They're waiting for fish to pass their stationary bait.

The steelhead is a very elusive fish which never goes in big schools. He's very wild and shy—never plentiful and never running like the salmon. I can remember the salmon coming up this river and crowding each other out on the bank. Never the steelhead.

Our drift boats have a better chance than the plunkers because we might cover ten miles of river in one day. We float from one hole to another and anchor at the edge of the hole and throw our bait or lure in with a lighter lead on, maybe a half ounce. That lead will bounce along on the bottom and you can just feel it tick, tick along the bottom. Your bait drifts down in the current to the fish that might be resting in the pool.

You stand up to row using about eight- to ten-foot oars. You have to have a little muscle behind you because when you lean into those oars there's quite a lot of pressure. Of course, you don't row against the current. You row sideways and the current carries you into position.

Awful hard work! You take off about daylight. I don't know why. You don't usually catch any fish then. Maybe there'd be snow on the ground, but when you're guiding you go out every day anyway, in all kinds of weather. You get out there on a windy day in that big boat with four people standing up in it and you just about pull your insides out trying to maneuver that boat. You don't work eight hours a day. You start at daylight and you end up when you get home and get gas for your motor. In those days you had to get your eggs ready for the next day, and all your gear, and attend to your other business. But it's fascinating out there in the open and I enjoyed it very much.

The boats as we see them now have only been in use forty-five to fifty years. But Meyers was one of the first men who guided on the Skagit in 1933. In those days you didn't use any motor. Someone would drive you up to put the boat in to float down three or four miles of river and fish the various holes. Then you'd load your boat on your trailer at the end of your drift.

That was still the custom when I started guiding in 1951. I had a five-horse motor but I couldn't go upstream with that. But in 1962 I became the first guide on the river to use a big motor. That twenty-five-horse motor with detachable tank would propel a boat upstream ten or twelve miles an hour. That revolutionized things. When I started in 1951 I might see four or five other boats out on a good weekend. Now they're be seventy-five on the same stretch of water.

Steelheading has gotten more popular as the equipment has improved. Its evolution has been amazing. I can recall as a boy my dad telling about fishing for six- to eighteen-inch fall and winter trout in nice little eddies and hooking into one of these steelhead. He'd set the hook and that steelhead would take off and wreck all his rigging. People couldn't hold 'em then because they didn't have the right equipment. I was talking to an old-timer who used to go out in 1905, 1910 on a small river just west of here called the Samish where there was a three- or four-foot-high dam for floating shingle bolts to the shingle mill. Trout could jump over but they'd pile up by the dam. People would ride their bicycles out to fish there, but they didn't want to throw their lines too far out in the stream because those big fish would get ahold of 'em and they'd lose all their rigging.

These fish are strong. I've been told by the fish biologists that the steelhead is the strongest species of fish that comes up the river.

In the early days we had bamboo rods, Calcutta bamboo they called it, that they brought in from over in the Orient country. And our reels weren't near as good equipment as we have now. Also, we used what they called a Japanese gut line, very brittle, and you had to soak it for several hours before you went fishing. When it dried out it was just like a coiled spring on your reel. So if you decided to go fishing tomorrow, you'd better take your reel and set it in a bucket of water overnight to soak up that line. Otherwise you couldn't cast it much over twenty or thirty feet. Also, the Japanese had a braided silk line, which was very expensive, and a braided cotton line they called cuttyhunk line, which wouldn't cast very good because it would soak up water. I can recall being amazed by the first nylon line after the war. It completely revolutionized fishing.

In the early days the only thing we used for bait was salmon eggs. We'd take cheesecloth and put the eggs up in a little bag we'd call strawberries. You cut a two-and-a-half-, three-inch square piece of cheesecloth, put some eggs in that, pulled it together, tied it, cut off the end, and it'd look just like a strawberry. About the size of a filbert nut or a little bigger. You'd put that on your hook and the fish would bite it because steelhead, being a trout, a lot of times will get behind where the salmon are laying their eggs and eat them. Of course, nowadays we also use lures with bright colors.

I like the feel of the bite. You fish maybe all day and you're feeling this sinker bouncing along in the water and all of a sudden it doesn't feel right. You feel a little bit of a tug. Sometimes you feel quite a jerk. Other times it'll just stop and you'll feel a little bit of a springy action on there and you'll realize that the fish got your bait. There's no flags go up in the air. No lights shine or blink or anything. You've got to feel it and very quickly jerk on that rod to set the hook into the flesh. So you have to be alert at all times for the bite. It's a challenge. I'm getting older and slower, but I wouldn't take my hat off to anybody on handling rigging and equipment.

A steelhead is a very difficult thing to land. There's no finer trophy fishing in the world. It's what you'd call the Rolls-Royce of sports fishing. You don't just hook a steelhead and drag it in and flip it into the boat.

You have to tire that fish out before you can land it. And if you have your thumb hooked on your reel too tightly, your leader snaps and he's gone. I've seen strong men sit down and nearly cry. They didn't realize that they were holding that fish too tight. I've seen steelhead jump at least four feet. Ping, your leader snaps and they break off and they're gone.

I can remember the first one I ever caught when I was ten or twelve years old. You could get a couple of dollars for a muskrat hide then and I had a few traps along the ditches and small creeks. One day I spotted a steelhead and chased it to where it disappeared under a bank. When I saw it again in the weeds and bushes at the edge I speared it with my trapping knife.

When I go out now I still have that same thrill.

Glee Davis

Ninety Years in the Mountains

Between the gold stampede of 1880 and the coming of the hydroelectric era in the 1920's the Goat Trail was the road to riches in the mountainous upper reaches of the Skagit River. Generations of men and pack animals knew its every scary twist and caprice. Glee Davis was five years old in 1890 when he and his mother first arrived in the country by dugout canoe and pack horse.

In 1880 a miner named Johnson described the original stampeders' trail as one of the worst in the world. Fifteen years later Glee Davis's mother, Lucinda, operated a roadhouse, or hotel, halfway along that route between the head of navigation and the claims way up on Ruby and Canyon Creeks. She recalled a winter return upstream to the roadhouse accompanied by young Glee. Travelling in deep new snow and camping overnight only two and a half miles from home, "We hurried all we could for fear of the [snow] slides. . . . We got to the midway point where the trail was blasted into the rock, afraid every second that the ice would break and fall." At an iced-over bridge they were almost stopped until Glee braced himself between the bluff and the bridge to forge a way through, this despite a steep drop to the torrent below. That was the way Glee Davis grew up along the Goat Trail.

"I'll go first," said Glee as he started down from the modern canyon highway, handhold to handhold, over scree, roots, and fallen trees, looking for the most notorious section of the sixty-years-abandoned mining trail. His old straw hat and green jacket disappeared in the brush.

We had not descended very far when we did come to a trail, a rough mountain track which obviously had seen much use. "Boy, the amount of horses that have come through here!" exclaimed Glee as he sat down to rest.

Later we mounted a small rise in the trail, and there in front of us across a rotten footbridge was the famous Devil's Corner, a point where the canyon wall jutted far out into the river channel.

The Devil's Corner's open-sided tunnel continued straight through the granite for about three hundred feet, a terror for the old pack trains. Glee passionately recalled a horse of his which had become stuck under the low overhang while carrying a tall cookstove.

The dilapidated steel cable bridge which we gingerly crossed had been laid over the miners' original log one in 1920 by Seattle City Light in developing a power dam. "Notice," Glee said disdainfully, "that this new bridge is sawed lumber, not the split lumber in our old one."

New or old, clumps of moss were growing on the weathered boards and brush had found a few rocky rootholds along the precipitous path. But despite its thick duff of fir cones and moss the Goat Trail's tread looked as if packers had not been gone long. In fact, listening to Glee Davis it was easy to believe that a string of horses might clomp by at any moment.

Rebuilding our old trail would be an awful nice thing to remember the miners who spent so many years up here working their lives out! But make the new trail the old way we built trails. Not too blooming good! Use split lumber instead of sawed lumber. And no wrought-iron railings. That spoils the beauty of it, to my way of thinking. Leave it the natural way that the rocks lay. Just throw out rocks and make a path. It seems to me that would be more appropriate. The trails I've seen lately, they grade them all out smooth so they can run a motorcycle over them. Of course, I wouldn't want to see motorcycles on any of it, myself. The motorcycles just don't belong in the mountains, to my notion. You're out there to hike and to take the things Nature provided, not destroy. The old trails were hard, hard on horses, but I like to be on an old trail if I can.

Just horses and backpackers. Well, fiddle, backpackers were the ones who built it. Tommy Rowland, for instance. Once he carried a load of five hundred pounds up the river to his cabin, what they call Roland's Point on Ross Lake now. He divided the five hundred pounds into four loads. He'd carry one forward, then go get another. He'd keep on trying to edge them ahead. Whenever I think of backpacking I think of that. Lately I heard kids talking about backpacking so I asked what they carry. I naturally assumed they were talking about carrying a load of freight.

Tommy was a better gardener than he was a miner. He was a wonderful gardener. An old Kentuckian used to call him God the Gardener since he was so religious. He lived by selling his vegetables to miners and he called his place New Jerusalem. He thought he was the Prophet Elijah and some of the miners had him committed so they could search his shack for gold.

In the '80's there was an old hermit here. Captain Randolph had been a steamboat man, but he ended up with a little shack here at the Devil's Corner. He scratched out a kind of trail around this cliff and charged a toll. Later in 1895 miners blasted it out like it is now. Quite a job! I've still got their time sheets. Each miner would donate a few days digging and blasting. There were about twenty men altogether. One fellow put in seventeen days. Another, William Jackson, had only put in one day when he was killed. They'd just blasted some rock, and Jackson got there first to dig away the rubble. He pried at the pile and it all came down on top of him and carried him into the river. Never found him.

They claim there was quite a storm of miners up here, maybe five thousand. But they overdo those figures. I located a number of claims myself. I was trying to find the Mother Lode, to see where that gold came from. Nobody seems to have any idea where it is.

When we first went up as far as Ruby Creek in 1898, sluice boxes were all over. You'd have a time finding room for a claim.

You can't make any money panning unless it's very rich. Hardly anyone did, and they went all over. I've sized it up that any colors have been ground

109

into flour. I never found any nuggets of any size. Oh, at the old price of seventeen dollars I'd find something worth twenty-five or thirty cents.

Yes, seventeen dollars an ounce! That was the price as far back as I can remember. In '93 we handled that litle trading spot at Goodell's. Handled it for two years for a prospector named Reese Jones. Miners brought a lot of gold down from the crevices along the Skagit and often paid us in gold. We had a little gold scale there. I still have a few little pieces of gold which they paid me with when I packed with my horses for the old Discovery. They say a fifty-dollar nugget came out of there. The one George Holmes had, I got a chance to roll that around in my hand. Like a small walnut.

I've been up to a place on Canyon Creek where they found a piece of old channel maybe sixty feet above the present creek. Well, the fellas shovelled the gravel out of that old bedrock and sluiced it down to the creek to their sluice boxes and they cleaned up three thousand dollars there.

It's very rich about a quarter of a mile above Ross Dam on the east side of the river. There was a box canyon there with straight walls maybe three hundred feet high. Well, there's pretty close to four hundred feet of water on top of it now.

There's lots of gold in the Skagit. Some pretty rich strikes! There's a wonderful rich place under a big pool above Diablo Dam. Two hundred feet under water. I had a claim located there at different times and took up some gold, but it never paid. Old George Neal and Andy Seawright worked that several different times and got quite a lot of gold out. You see, it came down from J. J. Jones's claim down through the canyon, around Sourdough, and dumped there in that wide place. Their gravel was not more'n a couple of feet above the water level and when they would dig down they couldn't get anyplace because it was all porous. Big rocks. They'd dig down and capture all they could. But the gold is still there. They never got down to the rich part.

Those old prospectors had a pretty hard life. But they were happy. Always thinking they were gonna strike it rich. Some did quite well, but they'd spend it on more prospecting. They wouldn't quit when they got a strike. There's more of it out there, so back they'd go. You, too. It wouldn't take you more than a day or so if you found some and you'd be saying, "I want to go and try that strike up there."

My own life seemed to fall to packing. I didn't like the job. My motto on packing is that it's only fit for an Indian and he's too smart to do it. But you do what you can to exist. I was a good packer and I'd always get pulled in on that.

Sometimes the income up in the mountains was pretty lean. In a way we'd have been better off someplace out near civilization, but my mother got awful stuck on the hills. I did, too. I lean very substantially to the woods and mountains. I just love to look at those rocks and to climb them, searching for footholds.

I lived so much of my life on that trail, running pack horses over it all the time. I had kind of a hard life—yet I wouldn't have missed it for anything. You know, I went barefoot a lot. Well, fiddle, I'd be packing in those mountains and just feel so good I'd take my shoes off.

Bill Tilly

"It takes fifty prospects to make one mine"

Born in 1906, Swedish immigrant Bill Tilly began working his Tilly Mine in 1947. He singlehandedly blasted and shovelled out about a mile of hardrock tunnel there and probably an equal amount elsewhere in Idaho's Purcell Mountains.

One summer day after an arduous hike up Hell Roaring Mountain I spotted carbide-helmeted Bill working beside his cabin and snow-roofed tailings pile. Being quite deaf from decades of drilling and blasting he did not hear my greeting until I was standing beside him.

His cabin was tidy but spartan. Scenery was its only luxury. From the window above the sink the old miner could look out across the densely wooded valley to a series of seven-thousand-foot mountains.

Tilly's horn-rimmed glasses accentuated his look of clean-shaven seriousness and mackinawed, rubber-booted practicality. His accent was as heavy as a pile of rubble, and he was short enough that he probably never needed to stoop much in his own tunnels.

The portal of this mine had recently caved in, halting the work, and Tilly was planning to move for the winter to his Bethlehem Mine a few miles westward. "Winter is the best time to work in these mines," he said. "They're wettest in summer and driest in winter." In fact, as we looked at the pitiful earth-filled opening a good-sized brook was gushing out between the ore car tracks.

The snowbound rockpile conditions of Bill Tilly's underground life would amount to a sentence of hard labor for most people. Yet despite never having produced any commercial ore deposits after decades of dogged, skillful tunneling, he denies any discouragement, because his claims are his own and he likes developing them. Desire is sometimes its own reward, and work, like beauty, is always in the eye of the beholder.

H ell, it's working for yourself. You ain't going to do this kind of work for wages. It's your own. And there's always chance. It takes fifty prospects to make one mine.

I was born and raised in Sweden and came to Canada in '28 and over to the States the same year. A couple of years I worked in the woods around Priest Lake. The Hoover Depression started then and things got so tough you couldn't get any jobs. So I started working for a prospector in '31 or '32, an old-timer named Swen Anderson. He just gave me mining stock for my work. And I located a property, what they call the Silver Crescent. I was the discoverer. Nobody had ever stuck a pick in the ground there when I found it in '32. It's down over the hill at Camp 9. The Silver Crescent was the only one I located by myself. I kinda got the Bethlehem on a trade for some rails and a mine car.

Mining was the only work I could get in the Hoover Depression. I came alone. All my folks are back in Sweden. I came to see the world. I could make more money over here, and I figured in a few years I'd save enough to go back and buy a farm. But I never went back. Three brothers and three sisters are all living, all married. Kids of their own. I'm the only black sheep.

To locate a mine you walk around looking. Most veins break out on the surface somewhere and some rocks, what they call floats, will break off from the vein and slide down the mountainside. You find them on the

surface. And often you find rocks or floats where uprooted trees have pulled them up. If it's any good, you file a claim. Locate it.

I drill my holes by hand and load 'em and set 'em off. No, it ain't hard. Mucking is the hard work. Shovelling and wheeling it out. Drilling is easy when you get used to it. You start in with a short drill. The last one is four or five feet long.

This lower one is a big working tunnel, five by seven. I made about a foot and a half a day drilling it. Just four or five months in winter. One hundred fifty or two hundred feet each winter. But now I'm on pension, so I'm here year-round.

It's about sixteen hundred feet plus about four hundred feet of cross tunnels. She caved in in the portal last spring after I left. I don't know whether to dig it out because if they make this a wilderness area, it would all be for nothing anyway. I'm just gonna wait and see. If I quit here, I'll go over to my other property, the Bethlehem Mine. If that turns out to be a failure, then I'll go out to find a new one.

The vein here was running north and south and this tunnel went straight into it. The other tunnels hit it, too. There was some good ore there but not enough to pay. You've just got to keep a-digging till you find a big enough deposit. That's development work. It's mostly luck.

It's fun. It's a hobby. When Swen Anderson started prospecting he asked Curly Jack a lot of questions about whether prospecting was any good, how he liked it, things like that. Curly Jack told Swen, "I'm seventy-two years old and I've been prospecting all my life and I never made a dollar, but if I had to live my life all over again, I'd do the same thing all over." And I feel the same way, too.

You work your whole life and never get nothing. It's interesting, though. I could have made good down there at the Silver Crescent if that partner of mine hadn't got it all balled up. They took out a lot of ore there during the last world war. This could be a mine here, too, unless they make it into a wilderness area. If they do, I might as well quit because I can't work the deposit from up here. To make a mine of it I'd have to start a tunnel from down below to haul the ore out and drain the water. They

116

can't take away my claim and steep road, but I've got to have a new road down below to work it.

I have a pension now and I stay up here doing this. It's hard work but it's better than hanging around town doing nothing.

I like to get to Bonners Ferry once in awhile. It's hardly changed over the years except for the wooden sidewalks and a few buildings. But then I get tired of town after two or three days and want to be back out here.

Tunnelling is about all I do except for housekeeping, and maintaining my tools, and cutting and stacking wood for winter. Oh, I get some visitors up here in hunting season. But in the thirty years I've been here I only know of two people who hiked up here from below. One kid was picking huckleberries, and then a fella with a cabin on the river had seen my light and got curious and came up.

When I started in there were quite a few prospectors around here. They're all dead now. I'm the only one left in this part of the country. But there are a lot more mines to be located!

Harte Pentilla

Snow Geese and Salt Marshes

In northwest Washington the Skagit River empties out of the Cascade Mountains onto a coastal plain called the Skagit Flats. Near the village of Conway the state maintains a marshy tidal stopping place for enormous flocks of migrating ducks. Elegant white snow geese, the famous "Skagit snows," winter over at Conway before returning to their spring nesting grounds on Wrangell Island in Siberia.

During any early spring visit to Conway the whiteness of the snow geese brightens the drab expanses of mud and dead vegetation. Loud goose voices anticipate the coming Arctic migration. Red-winged blackbirds tootle territorial calls from the catkined branches of greening alders. Towhees hop and flutter in brush along murky tidal sloughs. Amongst the old cattails long-billed marsh wrens gurgle the secret of where they will build their hanging nests. A female marsh hawk falls from the air to catch and eat an unwary rodent. Ike Island rises blue and helmetlike from the water. Doubly faraway Mount Erie slips out of the misty horizon. The season swells in the vibrant epaulets of the red-wings and in the dark shoulders of the four-foot-tall great blue herons. Everywhere invisible currents pulse with a force which is our greatest link with the past.

118

The American continent, which in the eighteenth and nineteenth centuries offered an inexhaustible treasure house of furs, ores, trees, lands, and waters, is now crammed with people and their competing demands. Today the question of how to husband the formerly boundless resources is one of the most important public policy issues facing our country. Ducks are a case in point.

Harte Pentilla is an affable, homespun man who was once superintendent of the Conway Wildlife Recreation Area. Conway is not a state park, he explained one fine autumn day. "This place began as an area where the unattached, non-club hunter could hunt. We used to call it a Game Range." He said that two hundred acres of oats, barley, and corn are grown to attract and feed the migrating geese and ducks. And as a public service pheasants are reared to supplement the wily migrants. Chuckling slightly, he described the pandemonium among the hunters as they crowded in to shoot pen-raised pheasants which had been released into the fields the night before.

Harte Pentilla is a traditionalist bird-dog man to whom the old hunting ways are very important. But although he knew that the public deserved something better at Conway, he was reluctant to press his own views against the demands of the slob hunters ("yuks") and released-pheasant men.

Traditional hunting was the original purpose of this refuge, but when you go out here to shoot ducks in the traditional manner you'll have lots of interference from people walking around. When I first came I used to shoot thirty or forty ducks a year. Last year I only shot two. Too many people. Too much shooting. Too much movement. Or birdwatchers, for instance, and they have just as much right to be out there as the hunters. Of course, you can't birdwatch either if the birds are being disturbed.

I think nonconsumptive use is going to be the future. Nonconsumptive use is people who don't harvest anything except a memory or possibly a piece of driftwood. I think Conway will have an interpretive center some day. Actually, throughout most of the year there is very little conflict between the hunter and the nonconsumptive user. But the population explosion! Well, one person can't tell another person what his recreation's going to be.

But I think that somebody should start teaching tradition. We have groups trying to disarm the hunter and stop hunting entirely. Hunter behavior causes part of this problem. When you have, say, two hundred people on one hundred acres hunting released pheasants, everybody's dogs fighting and people arguing over who shot this bird or that bird—that's not quality recreation. It can't be, no more than it's quality recreation to go fishing on a lake on opening day with another ten thousand fishermen. But we can't tell this fella what his recreation's going to be. I don't play cards, but I can't tell my brother-in-law that he's a damn fool for playing cards. That's his recreation.

I think the answer is public education with emphasis on aesthetic value rather than upon potting or killing a bird or killing a bird and taking it home to eat. Like I said, if you want to eat ducks, go buy 'em in the market. They're a lot better. Ducks cover a lot of country—all the way from Mexico to northern Canada. They're probably the most heavily parasitized animal that we shoot, that anybody eats, is a wild duck. They have everything. Intestinal parasites. I've seen beautiful fat mallards with tapeworms. They have lice. You pick up a duck and invariably you'll see lice on it. But they're specific as to ducks, not the kind that get on humans.

Let me tell you what I like about hunting. For instance, watching your dogs perform. That's part of traditional hunting. Raising a good dog from a pup to maturity and watching it perform in the field. And actually enjoying the weather. It's kind of brutal to go out there and enjoy that cold weather when it gets fifteen degrees and the snow geese are flying.

But there's a lot of beautiful things to see in the salt marshes besides a bag of dead ducks. The plants themselves. Of course, maybe I place too much emphasis on the aesthetic value myself. Maybe I should have emphasized economy. Heh, heh. Because you have to buy your box of shotgun shells, pay six and a half dollars for a hunting license, and three dollars for a duck stamp.

I haven't even touched on the value of these tidal estuaries and intertidal marshes. The life that's there under the water like the Eastern soft-shell clam. We've got millions of Eastern soft-shell clams.

The migration around the first of November is really worth coming to see. You take an evening like last night's with a beautiful sunset, you'll have as many as a hundred thousand ducks come in to feed. It's really a sight. You would think that that many ducks would spread out all over the entire area, but they don't. They'll all land on one or two acres, and you can't squeeze another duck in. And they're hogs. The ones in the back will fly in front of the ones in front. You can hear them feeding for half a mile.

Evenings during hunting season hunters will be leaving the fields to go to their cars—we have a certain time they have to get out—and fifteen minutes later, here's thousands and thousands of ducks.

This is the last salt marsh in the state. It's all we have. There just isn't any other place to buy.

Gaspar Petta

Hard Times at Thirty Below

As a lifelong trapper in Washington's North Cascade Mountains, Gaspar Petta was a late participant in one of America's original occupations. For it was the search for furs even more than the quest for gold which was responsible for opening up the continent. However, by the beginning of this century the old mountain men were largely a thing of the past. Their epic profession continued only in out-of-the-way places where the animals held out and where local men trapping for a few weeks each winter appreciated the extra income which helped them to survive lean times.

The North Cascades are rugged, glacier-shaped mountains traversed by wild, V-notched valleys. So much snow accumulates there from moist Pacific air currents that the spring and summer meltoff cascades exuberantly through alpine gardens—hence the name Cascades. But no gurgling brooks or tinkling creeks enliven the winter trapping season. That is a time of frozen sounds, of the muffled crunch of snowshoes on steep, fir-clad slopes. That is when the sleek, dark pine marten takes bait with a fury.

Since 1972 an excellent highway has annually funneled hundreds of thousands of visitors up the main Skagit River route on which Gaspar Petta first entered the country in 1912. In that very different time of wilderness

122

hardships he became a North Cascades rancher and logger who was at home in the fiercest winter conditions. The Jasper's Pass area (misnamed for him in the present-day national park) is still so rugged that few summer visitors reach it despite today's nearby road.

What 1980's outdoorsman would consider spending winters the way Gaspar Petta did on the tributaries of the Upper Skagit? Deep, wet snow, endless hours of darkness, and blood-freezing cold were his daily challenges. In a country noted for difficulty of access he snowshoed a trapline which could take a week to traverse in bad weather. In 1920 he bought a cabin at the beginning of his line from an old man who had managed to catch only one marten there. Although Petta eventually had two of these low log huts, most of his winter camping was done in fixed tents or simply under the spreading boughs of fir trees.

Gaspar Petta had already passed away by the time I began the interviews for this book. I am grateful to the U.S. Park Service for allowing me to use Cy Hentges's interview.

At first I just had that cabin I bought from the old man. I camped the rest of the time under trees. Pretty rough! Two winters I stayed in a tent ten miles up Goodell Creek by a great big rock higher than this house with slabs and brush to keep the snow off the tent. I carried a stove up there on my back. You bet your life! That's what the young fellas don't like to do today, but that's what you've got to do.

But it was good money at that time. In six weeks I got $305 for eighteen marten. That was a good chunk of money. The last big price I got was in 1929 for two months' catch on Goodell Creek and Baker River. Fancy furs I caught in January, way below zero, when a northeaster blowed there for three weeks. I got $606 for thirty-seven marten and eighteen weasels just before the Crash.

Once I'd been going all Saturday and Sunday with no sleep on snowshoes along the trapline. Just four hours sleep. Boy, was I sleepy! On that trip I got nine martens. Five large and one medium and three small.

I used salmon for bait at first, but the game commission cut that out. Then horse meat. You could get a horse for five or ten dollars.

I didn't use no trail. I'd just go right through the woods. Nice country.

Lots of people get a thrill by climbing peaks. I don't. I go high but I like the brush. That's my hobby, bucking the brush. Yeah, bucking the brush!

I always carried a pack, frying pan, meat, grub for a coupla days on my back all the time wherever I'd go, because if I'd get caught in a storm, it don't bother me any. Just get under a tree and build a fire and be right t' home.

Here's a bobcat hat I made in 1915. A kitten. The moths have never gotten into it. Absolutely breathproof and rainproof. And here are my balloon silk clothes to wear underneath the wool. No cheap cotton! Balloon silk. You can't buy it anymore. It's waterproof, but it'll sweat you in this warm weather. And there's the wool I wear. I bet you young fellas couldn't wear that. Thirty-ounce wool! If I get into a blow, I put the balloon silk shirt over my undershirt, then I put the wool shirt over it, and then my big thirty-ounce wool shirt. Stand anything! Otherwise you're not gonna make it.

A fella asked me how I go through the woods in the second growth when the snow's on the trees. I says I got my hood to wear over my big shirt, see. I tie it down when I don't need it. Someone asked, Why haven't you got buttons here? Well, it's so cold that you can't button it. So I use strings. I can stand anything and go anyplace. If you ain't got these, ohhh, you're a dead duck.

People don't dress for the cold. I never froze a limb. I dressed for it. Well, two years ago, Mrs. Farrar froze to death over at Snake Creek. She got in a snowstorm over there and, by gosh, she never made it.

Going up rough places on the mountainsides I'd use small snowshoes and drag the big ones. With big six-foot snowshoes in the right kind of snow you can really travel. Almost like skiing on crusty snow.

I was snowshoeing one time at Jasper's Pass when I started a snowslide. I had got pretty near to the top of the pass to where just a few more feet and I would be into the pass country and out of danger. I said to myself,

126

Thank God I'm at the top. Just as I said that, she let loose. I thought it was fun at first. Just a little snow let loose. And then it got bigger and bigger and bigger. It knocked me down, so I just sat down in the pack. Nothing I could do. Finally it got wide as this house here. It kept gathering more snow on the sides. Then it was going to make a turn. I said to myself, If she stays together, you'll be all right, but if she opens up, down you go.

Well, there was a rock, a great big one, and I was right in the center of the slide. The snow hit that rock. Half went to the other side and half went to this side. It stopped it. That was January, but the sweat was just coming off my head.

I went up to the pass again. But them big slides, that's different. If you ever get into one of them, they'll never find you. Never find a bone or a part of you.

Harvey Manning

A Step at a Time

Once I was visiting a U.S. Park Service ranger station with famed hiker/conservationist Harvey Manning to get a wilderness permit for a North Cascades trip. We overheard some other hikers asking about a certain backcountry trail. As is often the case, the Park Service employee did not know the answers, never having been there. The hikers then turned to us as fellow travellers and Harvey described the route in great detail. They asked about another possible trip, and another, always getting back an encyclopedic fund of trail talk. Finally one of them took me aside and, gesturing in amazement at my large, troll-like friend with the bushy gray beard, asked, "Who is that?"

The name Harvey Manning is synonymous nationally with back-country travel. Harvey is—when he is not hiking—a full-time writer of a whole shelf of books with titles like Backpacking: A Step at a Time *and* Footsore Around Puget Sound. *As a longtime conservation leader he has been instrumental in the fights to preserve the North Cascades and a mountainous urban park within sight of downtown Seattle which he named the Issaquah Alps.*

Only a true Puget Sounder would claim that he misses the rain when away from western Washington. Harvey's zest for his mosses and mists and dews is perhaps a legacy of having been a Camp Parsons Boy Scout almost fifty years ago in the Olympic Mountains.

Following forest and mountain blazes is at most an afterthought for most Americans, however uprooted they are otherwise. "But for some people," says Harvey Manning, speaking for himself, "going hiking is the only way they can keep their sanity."

I first started hiking in 1938 as a Camp Parsons Boy Scout when I was about twelve years old. By 1948 I was climbing in the North Cascades with the Mountaineers. I remember that there was a different style of hiking then. Mainly we expected solitude, to be alone. You didn't have to fight for it. That's why it's been very hard to adjust to modern times. Now those of us that have been around for a while, we usually can find solitude if we look hard.

At least we could until the past couple of years. But twenty, fifteen years ago solitude just came automatically.

Well, the backpacking fad seems to have peaked out. Equipment sales are declining. Most people don't stay at it very long anyway. That's always been true. Even a lot of my good climbing buddies of the '40's and '50's don't go out at all, don't go camping. People generally only stay with an outdoor life for a few years.

Lately the rigors have been so lessened by modern equipment that a lot of people have gotten into it because it's easy. It used to be that you went out without any shelter, and if you were three days from the car when a storm hit, you could be soaked every minute of those three days. That sort of thing tended to keep the crowds down.

People tend to stick to it if as children they got used to mosquitoes, being thirsty, hot and rained on, scared, and so on.

Everyone when there was solitude used to have self-reliance. We knew we weren't going to see anybody, so we were dependent on our own resources. There were not any backcountry rangers then. In the Mountaineers we had our own rescue patrol system. We took care of each other. But knowing that your buddies were back in Seattle ready to rescue you

in three or four days was small consolation. When you went out climbing that preyed on your mind, although you didn't talk about it a lot.

My big objection to Outward Bound is that it takes people who don't deserve the innermost secrets of the wilderness, and it takes them right into those secrets, ruining everything for other people. I don't think a person has any right to come from the state of New York, never having known anything about the Cascade Mountains, and merely by having signed up and having paid his six-hundred-dollar fee, to be led into the very heart of the inner core of the Cascade wilderness. That is something I think a person should earn over a number of years. You've gotta pay your dues. You should first of all know where the Cascades are before you get led into the middle of them, and these guys don't. These Outward Bounders would be just as happy in the middle of Iowa if they were told that's where the action was. They don't know where they are, so take them off into a corn field!

I'm not the elitist to say that they have no right to go into the mountains, but they should go into the accessible mountains. Then they can begin to wonder about the innermost part. Leave a little mystery there, for crissakes. When they deserve it, then they can go.

When we boys went out on those trips at Camp Parsons in 1938 and '39, although we were rambunctious and noisy, about twenty-five of us in a bunch, we didn't bother anybody. In the Olympics of that period maybe three-quarters of the use was by Scouts. We're all very loyal, anybody who came out of that generation of Parsons. There never was a better time.

That's not merely because we were young and that everything was new. It simply was the best of all possible times in our mountains, they were so pure and undefiled. There were no threats to them then because logging stayed in the foothills until after the war. I mean everything has been downhill since the '30's.

The Parsons system for getting little twelve- and thirteen-year-old kids to travel enormous distances up and down mountains was to give him a very light pack and very little food. You weren't going to starve to death, but you were going to be hungry the whole time you were out. If you were out for four days, you were hungry for four days. And you carried very few clothes.

Typically you'd come over to Parsons all prepared, or so you thought, for a hike. Your mother might have sent along long underwear and three sweaters and so on like that. Well, those people over there knew that all that stuff was going to end up on the Scoutmaster's back. So you'd lay out the gear that you planned to take on the trip and they'd start throwing stuff out. You're not going to take that and that, they'd say.

We were required to have nailed boots. Most of us had slivers, little chunks of iron you pounded into the bottom of the sole. In the course of a hike you'd lose half your slivers. Some kids had hobs, and there were a few rosebuds and caulks, too. You had to have nails because you travelled on snow.

Oh, and short pants. We always wore short pants, and that's the only thing I'll hike in now in the summer.

One other article of clothing was cotton pajama bottoms. You were always required to wear pajama bottoms for travel on snow because if you didn't have cover for your legs you'd get a horrible sunburn up on the glaciers. You wore them rolled up underneath your shorts until you needed them. We were very colorful on the snow, except nobody had color film in those days. Oh, and I had a shortsleeve cotton shirt and a light poplin windbreaker and a stocking cap.

We had no first aid kit, no flashlight, none of that stuff. No Ten Essentials. A toilet roll, that was the extent of your essentials. You had one essential and a cup and a spoon. All the cooking was done in Number 10 cans, so there was always a Number 10 can tied on the topside of your pack. The food was very minimal.

Lunch was a very good meal, like what we eat now. The standard Camp Parsons lunch was pilot bread, cheese, chocolate, and raisins. Breakfast was oatmeal or farina and prunes, and cocoa. Dinner was rice and tuna or rice and salmon.

Of course, the rice in those days was no quick-cooking rice. At five thousand feet it took about an hour and a half to cook a pot of rice. And you had to stir it constantly the whole time. Half would end up burned.

Half would have gritty little centers. A disaster. So the food was terrible except for lunch. But you were so starved that you'd devour everything you got. But that's how we covered long distances, by having light packs. Of course, you were cold at night so you went to bed as late as possible. There were no campfires since, with all those Scouts, we had to conserve wood for cookfires. We had no warming fires. As soon as supper was cooked the fire went out, which left three or four cold hours until dark.

So you'd go for an after-dinner hike to keep warm. We'd hike all day, have dinner, and go hike some more. When it finally got dark you'd crawl into your wool sleeping bag and, since it didn't keep you warm, you'd shiver all night. Unless you were down in the woods in a valley. You could sleep warm there. But up at five thousand feet you'd shiver all night.

When I was a boy the tents available in those days were too expensive for us. And anyway, they didn't work. We didn't even carry tarps because there was nothing worthwhile. We depended as much as possible on the old system of trail shelters.

Mainly we just hoped for good weather. If it rained we got wet, so we learned how to use trees for shelter. There's something called a tree cave, especially in alpine-type trees with spreading branches, where it's usually dry underneath. Well, we were very alert to things like that because you could keep dry in most rainstorms. Of course, in heavy storms everything got wet. We paid more attention to the weather than people do nowadays.

I got a tarp when War Two came along. A surplus seven-by-eleven life-raft sail with grommets. Orange on one side and blue on the other. That's all we had in Mountaineer camps, life-raft sails being used as tarps. There were just tens of thousands after the war, and we latched onto them for a couple of bucks apiece. I used a life-raft sail for ten years before it gave out.

When you'd get up to ten thousand feet on Mount Rainier, at High Camp, you'd pile up a little windscreen of rocks and you'd burrow in behind that and crawl in your sleeping bag and wrap up in the life-raft sail. That was your shelter for climbing Rainier. It was much more practical than a tent because all a tent does is just flap like hell. The wind is usually blowing forty to sixty miles an hour up there. Tent just flaps all night!

I'm not interested in tinkering with equipment. I want it as simple as possible and I don't want to spend any time with it. That's why I kept using the Trapper Nelson so long. By the time I gave mine up the Trapper had just about disappeared from the scene.

The Trapper was dependable. The first aluminum frame packs always were busting in the field and then people had to carry them out in their arms. I took many years to convince because I knew the Trapper wasn't going to fall apart. It was just a wood frame with two horns. You put your toilet roll on one of 'em.

Its advantage was in its curved slats which molded it to your back. Your back rested against canvas, and then there were a couple of canvas straps to put over your shoulders. But it really did punish your back.

But I liked the simplicity. That's why I don't own a tent. I don't like tents at all. There's only a rare occasion in these mountains when a tent is necessary, when you get a sideways-blowing storm, and you're in for an uncomfortable time.

Anyway, I just don't like to sleep in a tent. I guess it's the contact with Nature. I don't go to the mountains to get away from the mountains.

Les More

"We wanted to build a house"

Our historical right to own land has been as much a part of the definition of America as more abstract notions of freedom. The prospect of a place of their own was what drew most of the immigrants across the seas.

But when the first settlers arrived in the land of promise they had to build their own houses or enjoy an unhealthy amount of fresh air. For most this meant a log cabin, a structure which is part of American folklore.

Although technically there are many ways to build with felled trees, attitude is the most important factor in success or failure. Les More, for instance, has a strong commitment to her family and to creating a better future in the foothills of Washington's Kettle Range.

Les and Gary More are known among their friends as people who are willing to experiment. When a plague of grasshoppers devastated Ferry County, their garden survived handsomely because of its ingenious "chicken moat." But for several years their albatross-like log house project threatened to sink even the Mores.

Affable 35-year-old Les loves to show off her enormous log home's great open, juxtaposed spaces, its two bedrooms, two-story central area, and above-ground cellar. Her house draws a homey feeling from its rich, light-brown

135

tamarack and from its fieldstone fireplace and rear wall. But there is something improbable about it, too, as if someone's wildest Tinker Toy fantasy had been realized. Gary explains that "we didn't just sit down and come up with this floor plan. It evolved. We started with one room, and it just evolved into this."

Les, Gary, and their two small sons moved into the incomplete $12,000 dream house in 1978. That they managed to erect its massive larch walls the previous winter, working alone with a borrowed tractor, is a tribute to the strength of the old pioneer vision of home and hearth. That they survived their first winter in their rustic palace only helps to reinforce their reputation for pluck and innovation.

Les had met her husband in Oregon at college. Later, because both she and Gary had hated their five Navy years in Los Angeles and Chicago, they had saved every penny to try to live a completely opposite life—as homesteaders in the Alaskan bush.

June 1978

B ut I think we got a little bit scared after reading about Alaska. The difficulties, high costs, no jobs, isolation. And when we came here the laundromat was for sale. That was the kind of business we wanted, one that we didn't have to be there every second, like a grocery store or a restaurant. We wanted to be with our family. After we bought the laundromat we looked for land. We chose the business first.

We bought our laundromat so that we would have a little bit of security. So we'd be able to build a house and put in fruit trees and know that we could still make the land payments if something happened out here.

We aren't trying to live completely off the land yet. We keep hoping that we can use our thirty acres more efficiently. Right now a lot of it is just sitting.

But gardens take a long time. Five years for asparagus. So a lot of people get excited about being self-sufficient, but on the fifth year they lose their land just when the orchard is beginning to produce. You've got to be sure you can make it in the first five or ten years before you can truly let yourself go and be self-sufficient. If you have enough money to go out and buy the land, God, that's great. But we didn't. We'll be paying on it for ten years. Maybe in ten years we can be self-sufficient. We'll see.

We wanted to build a house. We had never lived in a log house or actually been in one. We just felt like it was one step closer to nature having our house made of trees. The lumber that we did buy, the roofing and the subfloors and all that, we enjoyed searching out the small little lumber mills up in the hills and talking with those people and getting the wood there, rather than just dealing with the big commercial lumber companies. We had a real good feeling about the whole thing.

We made our own house. That feels good. We can't bitch to some construction company because they made a flaw. We made our own flaws and we understand why they're there. They don't bother us that much, but if they do, we can change them. If something doesn't work, we say that we put it up and we can take it down and fix it. That's kind of a nice feeling.

We had a tractor with a hay lifter that lifted logs up to about fifteen feet. Then we added a little boom to raise them another eight. We knew we had to get the walls up by spring when the tractor's owners would need it for planting. That was such an incentive that we worked hard every day to get done, even if the logs were frozen to the ground or covered by snow.

Oh, it was freezing. I drove the tractor because Gary had to be up to receive the log, sometimes notch it, and fit it. But the tractor didn't have brakes, and it was tricky to drive it with the baby on my back and the little boy sitting on my lap. The worst thing was trying to hold the tractor in place with the clutch while Gary was up there deciding if the log would fit.

Finally we got so high that we started carrying them. Like the rafters. We carried all those up there on the roof. They were heavy to carry, but we had a system going. We each took an end and carried the rafter logs up and hooked them over a roof support and pushed. We got so if I grunted, Gary threw his end because that meant I wasn't going to make it. I couldn't say I was going to drop it. I didn't know. And I had to give everything I had. The first couple of times I dropped it, and that left him with a log

on his chest. After that if he even thought that I was going to drop it, then he'd throw his end, too. They were just too heavy to be messing around with and fighting the vibration.

When we started building this house I was six months pregnant with the second boy. Up until the end of my term I was working every day splitting shingles and peeling building logs. God, it had to be the fastest birth in history— less than an hour. I was all muscle, and when it came time I had all this good pushing power. The baby catapulted out.

Now that a lot of our friends are just starting to build we lend things to them. We don't have much use for a draw shave now so we say, Why don't you guys use it since you're at that point in your construction. Even things like picks. You don't use them that much except for foundations and outhouses. Everybody's pretty good about returning things.

Our philosophy is not to be dependent upon any one energy system. Eventually our water can be heated by propane or wood. And water can be pumped by electric or hand and heated partially by solar and partially by wood. And the lights will be either electric or kerosene. We're trying not to depend upon any one type of fuel, whether it be wood, propane, or electric.

August 1979

Last winter we could get the inside temperature up forty degrees higher than the temperature outside. So if it was 30 below, which it was in January, we could get it up to 10 above. During January and February every night was below zero, so the house generally ranged in the high 30's and low 40's.

That was because our house wasn't chinked or skirted or weather-stripped, and all the warm air just went outside. We could feel the wind blowing our hair, complete with all the sound effects as it whistled through the walls. Which made things really cold and semi-miserable. A wind-chill factor inside on windy days.

We had a cookstove, a barrel stove, and the fireplace. The barrel stove was in the middle of the kitchen—which was really dangerous 'cause the kids kept falling against it and getting burned. But it was either that or abandon the house.

We burned twenty-one cords of wood, and we were still that cold. You spent your morning chopping wood for the fires. We had to set our alarm and go and stoke the barrel stove every two hours all night. We'd take turns, each person sleeping four hours while the other person did it on the other two two-hour periods. Every four hours you got up and stoked. When it got real cold, the week when it dropped to 30 below, we were getting up every hour and a half.

When we'd get real cold we'd take off clothes and go outside and just get freezing. Then we'd come in and it would seem warm inside.

To prevent cold feet we sprinkled a little cayenne pepper in our socks. It's great. I recommend it highly. But you have to learn how much to put in. If you put too much, your feet get so hot they start sweating. Eventually that gets very uncomfortable—like wearing plastic boots.

We wanted to go outside so much so that the inside would seem warm that we had less cabin fever this year than we had the other years when we lived in a warm place. We were always going out sledding and playing in the snow and just doing anything. We didn't feel that the outside was a limit because lots of times we felt colder inside. So cabin fever really didn't come into play. It was more that you just got so sick of stoking the fires with no effect. The cold wasn't so bad physically, but mentally, gee, it just wore you down. Knowing that every time you left you were going to come back to a house that was so cold.

I work mornings in the school here in a 68-degree room. Since I had to come home to a 30-degree room, I could never adjust. I ended up wearing sleeveless blouses to school so that I could try to compensate. Everybody else was wearing thick sweaters. When I always stayed at home, like Christmas vacation, I didn't feel nearly as cold because I didn't have to go through the extremes every day.

We used to sleep in sleeping bags, until they burned. The kids started 'em on fire. Then we just had a lot of blankets. We'd put so many blankets on that, God, you'd get up in the morning and your body just ached from the weight. We spent a lot of time in bed just 'cause it was warmer. It was great—nice winter activity.

Most people around here tend to go to bed a lot earlier in wintertime. Usually you're in bed about eight. Get up at seven. We really slept a long time.

Last November the pipes froze inside. So we had to haul water from the creek for everything all winter.

We used to have an outhouse, but we'd converted it into a chicken coop and all the perches were across it. When the toilet froze we had to resort to other methods. Since we live on a county road, we couldn't just go out in the front yard. We had to put a garbage bag in the toilet, and then when it got full we'd take it outside and it would freeze. When spring came we dug a hole and buried all of our frozen bags. It was really gross. Gross.

This summer we've had a plague. Very impressive. The coming of the end.

We could see the grasshoppers coming down the hills in back of us. They hit the drier areas first. And the hills in back of us are real dry, sandy hills. Every day they were another twenty feet closer. They came from both ends of the valley. The people above and below us were wiped out one by one. So we were hit from two sides at the same time. It was amazing. Most of them were busy eating everything straight down. But as you walked, some would take flight. The whole ground moved in front of you.

We don't even feed our ninety chickens. And they are huge, six-and-a-half pound chickens. A big chicken in the store is like three pounds. Our chickens are so stuffed with grasshoppers—I don't even know if they can digest them all.

April 1981

We still have grasshoppers, but nothing like that first summer. A lot of people were wiped out in 1979, and others discovered in 1980 how much more they had lost than expected because their trees and stuff didn't recover. Our chicken moat is working great and spreading like crazy. A lot of people are using them to keep insects down in their gardens.

This year we're just kind of finishing stuff. We're gonna put the greenhouse on this summer. All the windows will be doubled up next month. We're just trying to make what we've got tighter. We're not cold anymore. The outside's all been chinked now. We can keep the house at realistic temperatures. We moved the heater to a different spot in the cellar so that the wasted heat now will go to the greenhouse. This year we only used six cords of wood for heating and two for cooking.

Our goal has been to get away from some of the commercialism and to do more on our own, and not necessarily do it all on a money basis but part of it on a barter basis. And deal with the local people rather than the big companies.

Yes, I would do it again, and I would build with logs again. I would make some design changes and that kind of thing, but basically we really

There is a lot of variety in building with logs. As you get sick of one project you're just about done with it and you're on a new one. We're pretty sick now of chinking and we have a couple of inside walls left, but that project is almost done. We want to build a log barn next.

We're real pleased with what we've built. But we didn't think it would take this long—four-and-a-half years.

Lowen Chin

Family

Lowen Chin's story sounds like one of those dynastic sagas which are so popular with novel readers. His is an epic of generations of adversity, emigration, and development of a new country, from Imperial China to frontier and 1980's America.

After the Civil War, Lowen Chin's grandfather joined thousands of other poor Cantonese seeking wages in America with which to build a better life in China. That was the epoch of giant transcontinental railroad projects and of immense need for navvies, unskilled workers. Even today it is not generally recognized how much the opening up of the West depended upon Chinese labor.

Casual discrimination against Chinese immigrants was very common. As railroad navvies they were regularly assigned lethal jobs, such as tunnel blasting, which no one else would do. And white miners, fearing competition, sometimes ran Chinese placer miners out of the gold camps. Even Seattle had a history of anti-Chinese riots. But despite exclusionary policies across much of the West, the Chinese somehow survived.

Lowen Chin's grandfather became a road contractor and labor importer. He was not only the first Chinese in Seattle but also the husband of a Vashon

143

Island Indian "princess" by whom he had four children—including Lowen Chin's father, who followed the common pattern of working in the United States and returning eventually to China.

When Lowen Chin was sixteen he decided to seek a new future in America too.

If anything, he found fewer opportunities here than either his grandfather or father had. Yet his children, the fourth generation, are well embarked upon professional careers.

If this story were a supermarket novel, it would be pumped full of high-adrenaline adventure. But Lowen Chin's account of his family's search contains the true-to-life drama of a journey toward America's traditional promise of a better future. Lowen Chin at 70 is both a very traditional Chinese in his habits and values and a typical American in his personal example of self-betterment.

You are what you are. No matter what you do you can never change what you are. See, I'm Chinese. Although I'm over here for fifty years, I still can't change. Maybe some people do, but I can't. I'm a one-hundred-percent Chinese. The way we live—we still use chopsticks and cook Chinese meals. If you give me a steak and I eat it, a couple of hours later I'd be hungry again. But if you give me a cup of rice, it'll last me all day. My system is like that.

Young people think you're kind of old-fashioned, but old-fashioned has got its points. It all depends how you look at what's good and what's bad. Just like in our old Chinese customs we respect the elderly because they've lived longer and had more experience. I lived seventy-some-odd years on this earth and I've seen a lot of things that young people have not seen yet. As if I've been around that corner over there and have seen what's there. But you who are over here can't see that corner. I've been there. I know. It's experience in life.

My father was born here. My father was half Indian, half Chinese. It was a very long time ago. His father come over not by steamer but by schooner. A sailing boat. At the time he got here most people in Seattle, they are Indians.

He come because a long time ago there were hard times in the old country. So he looked for someplace to go to make a living. Then he came here to help build the railroad. First as a laborer, then as a contractor. He built a lot of streets in Seattle—like Jackson Street.

They told us it took more than three months to cross the Pacific in a sailing schooner. That's why not many women could make it. Also, at that time they believed the woman's place was at home. Earning a living is a man's duty.

My grandfather married an Indian who was related to Chief Seattle. She had my father and three other boys and went back to China with my father. I don't remember her, and my grandfather died when I was nine years old.

When I first come over I almost found my Indian relatives. When I went to their house on Vashon Island they were not home. All my brothers, they saw them, but I don't. Once I tried to find the birth and marriage records but they burned up in a fire at Port Townsend. So there is no trace to prove that my grandfather married an Indian girl.

In 1932 I come over from China right in the heart of the Depression. Sixteen years old. See, we had an importing store here. We lived in Chinatown.

At that time we didn't ask our parents questions. We just listened and if they wanted us to know something, they would tell us. We didn't ask questions because that would mean that we didn't respect them. But my father was more like an American. He said we could make our own choice. But the others would say, You have to do what I tell you to do. But my father gave us a choice—to go or to stay. I chose to come over here. I thought that if I was away from home by myself, I can do what I want. At home I had to listen to my uncle, cousin, or anybody older than I was.

It didn't come out the way I wanted. When I come over I find out that the Chinese over here is more stubborn than in China. When you go apply for a job they ask, ''What's your father's name?'' See, they want everything within the family. That's what I wanted to get away from.

When I apply for a job they say, "Oh no, your family got so much money you don't need to work here." They turned me down like that.

And on top of that, there was nothing a Chinese can do outside of restaurant and laundry work. That's why everybody live in Chinatown. At that time, in 1932 or '33, the only thing Chinese can do is open up a restaurant—if they got money. If they don't, they put up a laundry. Remember the hand laundries? I had a hand laundry. You couldn't go have a job anyplace. They'd take one look at you and no. Extreme discrimination. It was very disappointing, but I got no choice. I stay.

Before the war no Chinese work in the shipyard. If you go up to Personnel, they say nothing. They don't even look at you. Because you're Chinese, black, or anything. And the seaman's union—no such thing as Orientals.

In World War II they start drafting everybody. When they come back they got GI Bill. Then they go to school and everything. That's why they got a chance. I went to sea in the Merchant Marine. It was about the same as the hand laundry, but in the hand laundry I be my own boss.

After the war I get married. Dropped anchor. I worked different places. I open up a dry cleaners. Ten years. I been working in a kitchen before. I work in Boeing. And now I work for Hostess Cupcakes as a cleanup crew.

The Americans made a mistake. When they come here they foreigner, too. When you look back—maybe two generations. And now they say the foreigners come in and take their jobs. Just like when the first Chinese come here to build the railroad because the work was too hard for the white men. OK, when the railroad was finished and they don't need the Chinese anymore they said the Chinese would take their jobs away.

What could I do about the discrimination? Sometimes you've got to work your way up. Time heals everything. But the white men, the Americans, keep making that mistake. They are so intelligent that they go up to the moon and up to Mars and yet they can't see more than skin deep. Not because they don't know how. Just they don't want to. They think they are better.

Things have improved since World War II, but there's still a long way to go. You can't change it overnight.

146

I think I would do it all over again, even though I was disappointed when I came. The decision I make is my own. Maybe I'm young at that time. But I stick to it like a man, without turning back. You make your decision—-you face it. You have to face it. It is your decision. Nobody make it for you. You make it for yourself. That's the difference between a boy and a man.

My future is almost end, almost the end of the trail. No more future to get. The future is now. I live by the day.

Let's say it this way. I accomplished what I set out to accomplish— to gain myself freedom and yet not disgrace my family. I can lift up my head high. I give everything to my family, to my children. I put nothing ahead of my family or my children. If anybody go hungry in the family, I go hungry first. No matter what. And if anybody harm my family, he gotta answer me.

Where you belong is where you feel comfortable, where you feel needed. I belong to my family. My family is here so I belong here. I raise my kids here. But in my heart I still wonder about the changes back in China. Besides, my father and mother, they die over there.

I went back recently for a visit because I left there a long time ago and I wanted to see what had changed. Just like a salmon when they are young and they go to sea and they come home and die. I think the human race is like that. See, you must come from somewhere. So you've got to go back where you belong.

But everything had changed. It hurt to go back. I am a Chinese. Come from China. When you go home and they treat you like a foreigner and you are a stranger in your own hometown—that hurts.

Tom Drumheller

Sheepherder

The first Northwest Drumheller, Tom's grandfather, had come out to present-day northern Oregon in 1852 on the Ezra Meeker Trail. His subsequent sheep operation in the Big Bend country of the Columbia was expanded by Tom's father into a ten-thousand-head operation in Montana, Idaho, and Washington, producing wool and meat for the Chicago market. Unlike today with its fenced-pasture method, that was a time of seasonal migration to the high summer ranges (which were often located on federal lands).

For Tom, Jr., the sheep business had many frustrations: the untimely end of his Massachusetts education during the Great Crash of 1929; the hard times of the '30's; and the increasing unavailability of herders. Yet the great yearly migrations in the open air had their attraction, too. "From the time I was about ten years old," said Tom, "I helped on the drives whenever school was out. I always kind of looked forward to it, although I can't quite imagine why, now. It was hard work, and the dust was horrendous."

Transhumance, the following of herd animals to seasonal pastures, is an ancient way of life little known to contemporary Americans. Tom's souvenirs of the old Drumheller drives (such as his ready-to-roll 1906 camp wagon) symbolize the extinction of a colorful part of our national heritage.

148

Properly managed, though, the renewable resources of our Western mountains could still make range sheep a very valuable form of husbandry.

The best herders you can get are possibly the laziest men because they can push a lot of stock and keep 'em fat. And on a drive so many fellas that are eager beavers will push the stragglers right up into the band all the time and, of course, the tail end is usually the weakest animals and those that need to be given the most protection. I can remember some of our good herders that would kinda hold back. They always brought us out good, fat lambs. And these other fellas, the eager beavers, were the ones that you had to hunt sheep for all summer.

Some of the old-timers would keep saying that, by gosh, this was their last summer, but the next year you couldn't stop 'em from going back. In that beautiful country it's really a paid vacation for these fellas. Herding sheep up in that country isn't a hard job. The easier you make it, the better job you're gonna do. You've got to work with the sheep and not against them. Sheep will feed early in the morning, and if you'll get up and take them out, they'll go feed together and by nine o'clock come back wagging their tails behind them into the bed ground. Then you can go back to camp and sleep. But at four o'clock you'd better get out there again. That way you don't hurt the range any. These fellas that are constantly dogging the sheep can ruin a range in one summer that we'd been working hard to keep in good shape for years.

Basques were excellent sheepmen. Good sober boys. Very dependable. They knew livestock. The French Basques were even better than the Spanish Basques in that they weren't quite as hot-headed. The French were more easygoing and had more patience around stock.

A good lazy fella has it made as a herder. But you also have to understand sheep and not work against their nature. I think it took me a good many years to find out the nature of sheep. I used to get pretty excited when some heavy old ewe would cramp down on my toe, but I learned that it doesn't do any good to take it out on a dumb animal.

But I think that sheep are a lot more intelligent than people give 'em credit for. You know, they're supposed to be dumb, and if one jumps over a cliff, the rest will jump over, too. Well, I've never seen that, and if sheep were as dumb as they're supposed to be, we couldn't have been in the sheep business. In the mountains their herding instinct keeps them together. I believe that sometimes the herder causes more loss than the sheep would ever cause. If the sheep wouldn't cooperate with you to stay together, you couldn't begin to take a band into the mountains. They're not dumb by a long ways, and some of the herders we had could have had a little more intelligence, by golly.

When you're in the mountains the sheep will pretty much work themselves in a good feed basin. But for moving them you need a good dog, especially one that's a backtracker, one that'll go back to look for strays after he's brought a bunch in. A dog like that is pretty valuable. The worst thing that happened during the war, when pool hall bums were the only herders we could find, was that they'd get up there and they wouldn't know anything about handling a dog, and it was really the dog that was herding the sheep. Some of those fellas didn't have enough brains to know that the dog knew more than they did, and they'd get mad and shoot the dog. We lost several dogs that way during the war. Of course, you don't pick those dogs off a tree anywheres, by golly. They're pretty hard to find.

Nearly all our bands in the hills would have one or two top older dogs with a pup to train. You have to train a lot of pups because there's always dogs that get poisoned or a rock rolls on them or some darn thing during summer. You'd be surprised. We used to lose a dog or two every summer, in spite of the dickens. And they get into fights and get crippled up—things like that.

So the herder would usually let the pup go with the old dog to start with, and then he'd hold the old one back and whistle and send the pup alone. Well, sometimes the pup would do a good job and sometimes he wouldn't. But it doesn't take long for them to learn.

We taught whistle or spoken or sometimes visual commands. Sometimes it was in English, sometimes Spanish, and sometimes Basque. So if a dog was, say, used to an American herder and he went out with

Tom Drumheller

a Basque, the dog would just stand there not knowing what to do until he learned the Basque commands.

Usually the dogs are taught not to get too close to the sheep. Very seldom do we have any need for a dog that will go out and bring one or two sheep in or out of a group like they do in some of these dog trials. The main thing is that if you're standing in a basin and the sheep are scattered all over the hillsides, you send the dog up and he'll stop and look back at the herder. The herder will send him on, and the dog will go a little farther and stop and look. But he stays way above the sheep all the time and just turns them back, is all. Usually, if you do that about seven or eight o'clock in the evening when the sheep are just starting to get filled up and some are just starting to lay down, that turns 'em and they'll just work their way back. And that's the way to handle a range. But these fellas that send a dog around and pretty soon they've got the whole band coming down in a big roar, well, that can tear up a lot of country. You don't keep a man like that, by golly, if you can help it.

In the early days we left Ephrata with a pack string about the first of June and started to the mountains. We were like nomads, by golly. We'd take off for where the grass was greener. That was about a ten-day trail, making an average of ten miles a day with a band of ewes and lambs up over the Big Bend country, which was all wheatland in those days. Marginal wheat country. We'd go maybe two or three miles through lanes with wheat fields on each side and then maybe we'd have a whole day's drive where we could spread out over a lot of unused land. Just plain rangeland. A lot of it belonged to the bank and to the U.S. Land Office. The country was not very well built up, even in my day, about fifty years ago.

The business of trailing the sheep to the mountains covered quite a few years. It was always hard work. You had to get up at three or so to get breakfast from the camptender, always a real good cook in those days, French, then Spanish Basques. Because in early June it gets light pretty early, by four o'clock we had to be ready to go. The sheep would be at the head of a lane. We'd filled 'em up the night before so we could handle 'em in the morning going through maybe three or four miles of pretty poorly fenced wheatland. Most of these farmers were operating on a shoestring anyway, and to build fence was expensive, so there just weren't many fences on the lanes. Walking about one to two miles an hour, by nine o'clock in the morning we'd have come to an open spot at the end of even the longest lane. We had those places pretty well lined out along the trail all the way up there. Then we wouldn't start on the trail in the afternoon until maybe four o'clock. During the middle of the day we'd sleep. The boys would get their bedrolls and just lay down in the middle of the day. Then at four o'clock we'd start out if we were in a place where we had an afternoon lane. But if we didn't, we could graze the sheep and that would make it a lot easier the next morning. But it was a matter of about ten miles a day for about seventy miles getting up to where we'd take the sheep across the river.

Of course, the other fellas' bands which came after us would range a little further from one side to the other on the trail, and some of them would range a little too far into the wheat fields. Then the sheriff would be out to see the fellas. Most of 'em would say those sheep belonged to some other sheepman. They'd never give the right man's name. We didn't have much trouble ourselves with the farmers in those days. You can't win if you don't get along with people. In those days no one was making a very good living. We were all in the same boat, and we got along a lot better when that was the case. When people get affluent they have a lot more problems.

The first year I was on the Pasayten River was 1926. Then I went back in '27. We had a Basque foreman who had come over when he was eighteen years old to work for my father and had been with us ever since. That summer I went down the Middle Fork of the Pasayten with him. There had been a big burn shortly before that, and the only way you could go was to take your horse right down the creek. The Pasayten was excellent feed then. All that fireweed was coming in. The fire had been clean on the ground, but it had left all those snags sticking up there. In about eight or ten years when they started going down, that was the end of the range in that area. But those ridge meadows, especially up on Buckskin Ridge between the West Fork and the Middle Fork, were excellent feed.

Good country for bears. Most bears won't bother you. Especially if the berries are good. I remember sitting in the Ferguson Lake Camp at the head of Wildcat Creek and looking down through that meadow and on both slides, the Silver Creek Slide and the Ferguson Creek Slide, and counting over thirty bears. The berries were good that year, so we never had any bear losses. But other years, by golly, we had thirty or forty sheep lost before we could finally get the bear that was doing it.

The herders I had! During the war they lost as many as seven hundred sheep at one time. But in order to find lost sheep you've got to get right on 'em the minute they're gone. If you don't get 'em within twenty-four hours, you might as well stay home. Because once a bear gets into them, or a coyote or lynx or most anything else, they're just gonna scatter.

Well, I don't see any future for range sheep and I don't think that the farm flocks will bring our numbers back up. We're under ten million now, and we were at fifty or sixty million when I got out of school. Prices have gone just the other way.

The only way to bring the numbers up is with range sheep, but federal lands have so many restrictions that there's no way in the world that you can operate. And, of course, when you have range sheep you have to have herders, and there's no labor that you can get anymore. There are few people left in the country willing to work as hard as we did. So there are very few sheepmen left that try to operate like a range outfit used to.

I hate to see that because we need to produce a few thngs in this country to make our dollar worth something again. People who went through the Depression of the '30's all have a kind of kindred spirit. We learned then what being frugal amounts to. Nowadays it doesn't pay to be frugal because if your money's not worth anything in a few years, you might as well spend it.

Paul Louden

"We'd whistle and sing to hold them cattle"

◈

What kind of man makes a career out of caring for large, smelly, sometimes dangerous range cows?

Paul Louden at 90 is one of the Okanogan's few remaining old-time cowmen, a direct link with the region's epic cattle period. "I was already riding as a cowboy when I was twelve years old," he boasts. And about his marginal grammar school background he says, "My education was good for what I wanted, which was to be a cattleman."

In the 1860's the Cariboo gold rush had attracted large cattle drives into the Okanogan, north central Washington's parched sagebrush hills and valleys. By the 1870's cattle dominated the Okanogan the way apple orchards do today. Paul Louden's father was an extremely enterprising sheep and cattle pioneer on that frontier.

After Paul's exciting youth as a cowboy, horse packer, and teenaged partner in opening up a remote tungsten mine, he managed some of his father's ranches, was mayor of Oroville (where he had a butcher shop), participated in Prohibition whiskey running, and ran cattle on the wilderness summer range of Chopaka Mountain.

Chopaka had cattle running on it when I was a very small boy. My father came into this country before I was born in 1891. He'd run horses up here and then he brought in about seven hundred head of cattle from Ellensburg. He swum that Columbia River twice with them cattle and never lost one of them. Calves and everything crossed first near Ellensburg and then near the mouth of the Okanogan River. At one time he had over three thousand head of cattle. But after I grew up we ran cattle out in the open out around Okanogan, Similkameen, and Loomis. We took the first cattle in that ever got way back in the hills over around what we called Big Camp in the Cecile Creek country. We'd take our cattle back there and turn 'em loose, see. Then maybe we'd have one man in with a thousand or fifteen hundred head to ride and put out salt.

Early in the season we drove them up close to Chopaka Lake. Pretty soon we'd move 'em back a little further, and then we'd move 'em again way back, clean back into Snowshoe Camp and all through there clean over to Horseshoe Basin. Then, of course, we'd go in every once in awhile to see how they was. And then finally when it come time to take the beef out we'd go back in there and gather them. Later in the fall we'd gather the cows when the snow began to show up. That's the way it was worked, see.

Sometimes we'd have good days and sometimes we'd have regular old blizzards. I've rode back in there and, God, it'd be cold as the dickens. Sometimes them cows wouldn't follow out like they should. Young cows would get lost. One time we'd seen six or seven head with an airplane so I sent a couple of Indians in on snowshoes to bring 'em out. I gave them a hundred dollars and they went in and brought 'em out.

Of course, in them days all the cattle were wild and had to be roped. Along in May we'd brand the calves born in the spring. Well, we'd take them into a big place and hold 'em up. There'd be you and another fella, say, was roping. I'd come in and I'd rope one and bring him along to my partner. If the calf was bucking like the dickens, I'd go slow and if he was digging his toes in, I'd go fast. Then that rider would come alongside, whip the rope under and get the calf's hind leg. Then they'd stretch him out and work on him, brand him, earmark him, cut him, and everything like that.

If the first fella had missed roping that animal, he would never stop. He'd continue along in the bunch and try for another one. Well, most of my time used to be heeling because I could outheel any of them, not to say I'm bragging on it now. But I could heel and I had lots of good ropers that knew what to do, knew how to pull 'em. Bad ropers would rope one and come dragging it along and you could throw a dozen ropes under there. He'd knock them out with his toes. His toes would never get high enough for a rope to get underneath.

There's lots of tricks in it. I taught lots of fellas how to rope good, how to hold a calf.

Oh, in the rodeo I was awful good down in Ellensburg and that country and they got so that they wouldn't let me rope anymore and they made me one of the fellas to announce the winners. But I was taking my share of the money and a hell of a lot more. I guess it was something I liked and it was natural for me.

Other calf ropers would ask me how in the world I got my horse broke the way I did. You must beat the devil out of him, they said. Well, I never did. If they was the right kind of fellas, I'd tell 'em how to do it. The main thing where you're roping for money, your calf comes out running fast trying to get away. Well, what I did when I went out, I'd tip my horse just a little bit so the animal running ahead of me would see which side of him I was on. Then he'd turn away and I'd just pass the rope over his head. He'd just run his head into it, see. These other fellas, they'd rope 'em over the nose and it wouldn't go down over the neck and the calf'd be a-running and a-going like the devil and them fellas trying to shake it on. It was a long time before they ever caught on to how I was doing it.

But you don't see no team ropers roping and branding out in the open anymore. We'd bunch up maybe a hundred or a hundred and fifty head of cattle along a lake or someplace. There'd be three or four fellas holding 'em out there and them cattle got used to it so you could ride in the bunch. You'd hold the herd kinda loose so you could pick out the right ones. You didn't get them all, of course. No, I don't think there's any range ropers anymore at all. I've seen fellas try it since then but they didn't have the schooling to get the art of it.

First a beginner has got to know how to make a certain size loop according to whether it's a big or small animal. And leave some extra rope so it wouldn't jerk from the start and it would feed out all the time. Leave a little bit of extra rope behind the loop. Now if you was roping big, wild cattle, you'd use a bigger loop.

And another thing, a lot of fellas don't know how to dally with their rope. When your horse is holding the cow you loop the rope counter-clockwise around the saddle horn. If you loop it the other way, well, the first thing you know the rope'll catch your finger and burn it or cut it off. If somebody doesn't show you how to do it, you'll get hurt or burnt.

Also, a beginner shouldn't interfere with his horse if the horse knows more than he does. Say you've got the head rope. When your heel man catches the cow and you stretch it out, you've got to slack your head rope so the cow will go down on its side. Both horses turn and look right at it while they're doing that. And them horses, they get smart. Whenever the branding iron is put on to burn, naturally them calves or cows will kick. But them horses get smart enough that as soon as the iron's smoke hits the animal, they'll back right up. Because if they let him kick out, then they gotta go all through it again. By God, it's no time until a good rope horse'll learn how to do that.

When we had good rope horses and lots of saddle horses we'd each always take about five horses. We didn't just ride one day after day like they do now. We'd change horses a lot. Then we'd have these good roping horses who knew how to place theirselves and knew how to hold 'em after they got 'em. Them horses we hardly ever used for anything else. Just roping and separating or maybe if we was camped out on a big drive to Yakima or Ellensburg. Them horses wouldn't be rode in the daytime at all. We'd use them for a night horse, just standing around on night herd, maybe five hours a night. Then you'd turn that horse loose. But when you was moving a big lot of cattle like that you'd never turn your horse loose until you'd caught another one and put your saddle on it. Every cowboy, by

158

God, was supposed to have a horse ready to go in case of a stampede. Well, no, today they'd all get in bed with a kleutchman and go to sleep.

I was never in a big stampede because we always caught it in time. Dad was pretty goddamned foxy with us and there was no monkeying when we were out on night herd holding 'em. You wasn't allowed to light a cigarette because a quick light like that'd do it. Or a quick movement or anything. The worst time was during thunder. So then we'd whistle and sing to hold them cattle. And long's they could hear you they wasn't hard to hold. It'd take about three nights before they'd settle down. From that Loomis country you'd make about ten miles a day feeding and grazing along down to Ellensburg. About a seven days' drive at the best.

Every cowboy'd have a song of his own like "Hey There, Hi There." Some darned thing. They could see the trouble a-coming and they'd start to singing and whistling. Each one would patrol only one section of the herd so's he'd get to know what was going on there, if some animal was up and looked like it might move soon. They'd be a little spooky, them old rascals, until you got them quieted down. But if you ever got in a stampede on the first two or three days, you was in trouble all the way through. From then on all you had to do was let a fart out and away they'd go.

When my dad first come to the country he had seventeen hundred head of cattle and calves in one bunch. He started near Yakima with some men, including two good cowboys who knew what to do. Each time they came to a lake they'd swim the cattle across it to practice for when they had to cross rivers.

They had men here and men there on both sides of the cattle with lots of extra saddle horses. All horses was broke to swim in them days because there was no other way to cross rivers. If you wanted the cattle to travel faster, you'd close in on 'em. If you wanted 'em to slow down, you'd loosen up. To keep them from getting turned down the river you'd work them like that. And you had to have that water just right. Now if you done it early in the morning when the sun was a-coming up, a-sparkling on that water ahead, them cattle'd turn around and come back. So a river

crossing had to be before sunrise or after sunset. You couldn't go into the water in real sharp morning light.

There was a ferryboat about sixty or seventy miles out of Ellensburg where Dad's cattle got a good swim. He put a bunch of calves onto the little ferryboat; it'd hold a wagon and team. Them calves was a-bawling for their mothers and so them old cows followed in the water. When they got to Brewster they had to swim the Columbia again because of the way the river curves around. There the cattle just went in and swum right across. And when they got to the Okanogan River they swum that.

They didn't drive the cattle right at breakfast time. As soon as it begun to get light they'd ride through 'em and raise 'em on their feet to start grazing. Some fellas'd come in and get their grub from the cook at the chuckwagon. Then they'd go out again and the fellas that were night men would come and get theirs. After everything was set they'd start moving the cattle till they come to a good bunch of grass where they'd feed them awhile. When they'd camp for the night they'd try to get on a big open place where the cattle could see one another. Otherwise they'd stampede awful easy. If they were all together in one place and could see one another, they held that much better.

Each man had half the night to sleep. And in the daytime along about noon, pretty near everyone would get an hour or so of sleep while the cook and the horse wranglers watched the cattle. But the first two nights of the drive pretty damned near all of them were out and the only time you got to sleep was in the daytime. They had to be awfully careful at first because if the cattle ever stampeded once, that was trouble all the way clean through.

In these here movies they're all the time screaming and yelling and shooting and running them cattle and just tearing to beat the band. But you had to have a pretty good head on you to handle them cattle. They was much wilder and they had long horns on them. Ain't like now when they dehorn 'em, y'know. God almighty! Sometimes them big cattle would be sold to somebody and have to be rebranded. Well, they were big fighting cows and Durham cows with horns. But them good cowboys packed about a seventy-five-foot rope. Nowadays in these rodeos their ropes are only just about long enough to tie up their horses. But in the old days you needed a long rope because if you roped one of them big cows, it might take right after you with its horns. You had to have a horse that could get away. Well, there was two brothers I knew packed hundred-foot ropes. And they were awful good ropers, too. Big tall fellas. God almighty, they could throw a rope a long ways. Oh, the cattle were wild then!

Nowadays a horse won't get hooked. Just butted a little. Back then a lot of people got hurt and killed in stampedes. My gosh, you had to be careful. You couldn't just ride right in front of them and throw your hat at them or somethin' like that to stop 'em. You had to swing 'em in a circle. Two or three fellas'd be tryin' to swing 'em on one side while the fellas on the other side held back. And as soon as they'd turned 'em, they'd go through and cut off a little bunch and get 'em quieted down again. You bet it was dangerous!

Slim Worthen

Branding Iron Maker

Like most Methow ranchers Slim Worthen in his youth had learned enough blacksmithing to be able to do ordinary farm maintenance. But beginning in 1949 he went on to learn the proud art of working with metal, of crafting that all-important symbol of ranch life, the branding iron.

Brand lingo has its own conventions. For instance, "running" means written in script rather than printed. "Flying" signifies a letter or number with wings. And a "bar" appears as a straight line. The challenge is to translate all of these orthographic requirements into hard steel.

Although the purpose of branding is to identify ownership, especially on the open range, according to Slim Worthen a brand "is primarily for honest people." The dishonest can easily alter a brand or slaughter the animal and sell its meat.

Honesty, integrity, and hard work go together in Slim Worthen. He typifies the proud family farmers who once were the predominant class of Americans. Until a recent heart attack slowed him down he and his wife farmed and ranched with old-fashioned horse-drawn equipment. "We didn't use much equipment," he says proudly, "and there was little expense, so we didn't have to have a great big income." But he adds, "We took it out of our

hides, though, working out—she teaching school and me working in the woods."
Slim Worthen is a tall, direct-eyed, rawboned jack-of-all-trades, a brand of man
becoming all too rare.

In 1949 I began working at Rev Ansteth's machine shop in Twisp.
Ranchers and hobbyists would come in and want an iron. What we
didn't know we figured out. Originally Rev's had been a blacksmith shop
but as time went on they put in welders, lathes, and milling machines.

A lot of this blacksmith work is kind of a lost art. There was mining
and construction work where we'd have drill steels to sharpen. Now it's
all diamond drills. You throw 'em away and buy a new one. The same with
the ploughshares.

Even when I was a young man, why, all you needed for farming was
a footburner plough, a walking plough that you hitched a team of horses
on and walked behind. And a disc and a harrow. And if you couldn't afford
a drill, you could always seed your grain and grass and clover by hand and
harrow it in.

We drew a lot of ploughshares before the throwaway ploughshares
came in. Why, we had the old hard steel share that you had to heat and
draw, hammer out, and then temper.

But it can be machine-made so much cheaper now because the labor
offsets the material. It's machine-made and then tempered under strictly
controlled heat in ovens where they control it right to the degree. Doing
it in a blacksmith shop, why, you have to learn to guess when it's hot enough
and when to cool it. You can't compete with machinery.

I had to make some branding irons over when I first started. You see,
they have to be pretty precise. If a man wants to register a brand, why,
he'll write to the Brand Department and tell 'em what brand he'd like to
have. Well, they'll let him know if that has already been recorded or one
too similar. And when he's got his brand he'll give me the specifications,
height, width, angles, and everything. When I made my iron it had to
fit that picture.

My initials are W O W so I have a W with an O in the center of it. They call it a combination W O W. But it's not really the best brand. Any time you can get an open brand it's better. But there are so many brands registered it's hard to get an open brand anymore. By an open brand I mean one that the heat can escape from. If you have an N like Ross Filer's, why, there's no place to trap heat. But something enclosed, like a B or a P, you have to be careful branding because that might form a blotch. Instead of being an O, for instance, if you leave it there too long, it'll just be a big blob. A round dot.

I made an easy one for Gary Balesby over here. It's a U bar U. I made it in two operations. He uses two irons. It didn't take me a half hour to make that. You take steel, five-tenths of an inch thick by an inch and a half to two inches wide. You have to have enough material there to hold the heat. But then you grind the edge down, not quite to a knife edge, about an eighth of an inch at the face where you put it on the animal. So that takes most of the time. Well, after that was done all I had to do was bend a U and put a handle on it. And then cut a piece the length of the bar and put a handle on it. Well, he had a lot of branding to do so he wanted two U's. Two U's and one bar. That didn't take much time.

Another time we had a hard one. I remember Rev and I both worked on it in the shop for half a day or more. It was for State Representative George Zahn, an apple man who had a few cattle. He wanted a delicious apple brand with a Z in it.

Well, you know a delicious apple has five points on the bottom. Looking at a side view, three points show—one in the center and one on each side. Well, we studied on that for a long time and finally decided to put two quarter-inch plates on the anvil about a half inch apart. One of us held those hot pieces on the anvil while the other placed a shoty on them and hit it with a hammer.

A shoty is for cutting hot steel, sort of like a splitting sledge for firewood. It has a hammer on one side and an axe-shaped bit on the other side, wedge-shaped. But it has a handle. The idea is not to hit with the hammer end but to hit it with another hammer. The old-time blacksmiths used it a lot before they had cutting torches. Why, they'd get their iron

good and red- or almost white-hot with coal or Douglas fir bark, and lay it on the anvil, then lay this shoty on it, and hit its hammer. You see, you can cut real heavy steel that way when it's very hot.

We had a shoty that was kind of blunt but we didn't sharpen it. We placed it over the two steel plates which were about a half inch apart and hit it with a hammer to make the three little bumps, the delicious points. Then we made the center where the first bump was and formed it around in the form of the apple.

That was about the hardest one I ever made. The Z in the center was easy 'cause it was just three straight lines. You can get that two ways. You can cut short pieces and weld 'em together. But if you have a good forge and a hardy—that's a wedge-shaped deal that sets right down in a square hole in your anvil—you'd make a sharp bend with it. With an N or an M or a Z you'd make about a one-hundred-thirty degree bend. Because the hardy is sharp on top you can make a sharp bend. If you had a small piece of steel, why, you'd just bring it out of the forge and lay it across the top of your hardy and hit it with a hammer. Red, nearly white-hot steel is very soft and you can mold it just like plastic.

An old blacksmith told me one time that only two blacksmiths ever went to hell. He said one of 'em didn't charge enough and the other was pounding cold iron.

Foss and Bill Creveling

Cayuses

❖

"I got my first horse when I was four or five years old," says Northwest rancher Foss Creveling, crinkling his laugh-lined eyes. "And I've never been without one since!" Now in his seventies, Foss Creveling still raises cattle on a "rawhide" ranch in Washington's sage hills. He still walks with the bowlegged gait of a man literally raised in the saddle.

For most Americans the value of horses for life in the 1980's may be hard to imagine. Although mounted cavalry charges were used until early in World War II, horses' efficiency for transportation was outdated long before that. Possibly their only true believers today are adolescent girls and two-dollar pari-mutuel bettors.

Until machines finally replaced them early in this century, horses were everywhere. The word horsepower comes down to us from not so long ago when getting work done meant harnessing up a four-legged helper to do it.

"Get a horse!" cried the automobile's first critics, and no wonder. There was something infinitely more personal about pack horses than trucks, or about plough horses than tractors. This is not ersatz nostalgia but the reality that the horse, unlike a machine, reacts to us with pleasure and with anger. He has a personality. Moreover, his condition and character are a readily *understood measure of his owner's frugality or largess, folly or wisdom.*

Foss Creveling's horses are definitely working horses—schooled in the same range skills which young Foss practiced in early day Northwest rodeos. From long experience Foss and his son Bill can judge their horses' moods by the "fire" in their eyes. That type of concern is what we need more of in the eighties. In that sense horses and horsemen will never be outdated.

Although rodeo started way back, it's only been since the '30's and '40's that rodeo has been the professional deal it is now. We have more top, balanced riders today than we ever had back years ago. And they have a different type of bucking horse now than I remember. We had what they called a sunfishing horse. A lot of today's professional riders couldn't ride a horse of that type. You had to keep them old horses on their feet as well as stay on top of 'em. They'd fall on the ground. Of course, if you got mad enough at him, you could step in that stirrup heavy and pull him down and hold him there until he wanted to get up. We was riding smaller horses then and they were out of different stock, out of cold-blooded stock. There weren't many thoroughbred or hot-blooded horses until some breeders started importing them from England.

Wild horses were what you needed for a cattle camp because they were used to grazing out and wouldn't run for home. They were used to foraging for themselves rather than being fed in a paddock. All you had to do was catch one.

You just outguess him until you're close enough to get ahold of him. They're not really true wild horses but domestic stock that's been let go. And some of them's pretty independent and sharp because they've been running wild and been chased and whatnot. Usually you build a trap or a snare, corrals, or get him in with a bunch of your own horses.

Then you get him so you can get your hands on him. One of the better ways, and less abusive to a horse, is just rope him by the front feet. And pull his front feet out from under him and tie him down. Don't abuse him but show him you're not gonna hurt him and that you and him is gonna get on working terms. Now the old way was that when you kinda got him broke to lead and paying attention to you, why, then if you needed him real bad, you just saddled him up and went to work on him.

That's about as good a way as any if you need a horse fast, if you're moving stock or something or if you've got someplace to go. Saddle him up and take off. You might lose ground for awhile but the idea is to get him a-going your way.

If he starts the other way, get him to circling and leave offen the circle when you're at the point where you want him to go. He thinks he's getting away with something then, and you go off up the trail.

The big thing is to get the horse's confidence. Then he knows you're not gonna hurt him but he has to mind. Then you get on a pretty good working basis. He gets so he likes to do something that pleases you and he can tell whether you're pleased or displeased. You bet he does! People say a horse doesn't think but I'll tell you, if he doesn't, he makes up his mind awful quick!

The Creveling ranch is located on a high bench overlooking a valley of irrigated apple orchards. Above it on the dry, dazzling hills some of the Creveling horses were grazing under a cloudless Okanogan sky. All the cattle were away for the summer, up in mountains owned by the U.S. Forest Service.

The ramshackle outbuildings, the lodgepole corrals, and the scattered lariats, branding irons, hardware, and horse gear all fit into what Foss's burly son Bill described with a wave of his hand as "just a rawhide outfit." This was no white-fenced, elaborate tax-writeoff ranch but a working spread in the local homestead tradition.

Under the attentive gaze of three young horses Bill opened a pole gate and walked into a round corral where he demonstrated some roping techniques. He swung a rope clockwise around his old Stetson and released it forward onto an imaginary horse head. The rope raised little puffs of dust where it hit the ground.

Just around like that and over his head. By golly, around here you learn to do that by the time you're sixteen years old if you want to catch your own horse and go out with the boys. That's a head throw. Now a foot throw, if he's going around this round corral, you lay your rope right

out in front of him. He puts two feet in there and you tighten it right up. Then you can jerk that slack and set him on the ground. Tighten the rope around your waist and the minute his front feet land that's when you pull them right out from under him. Then tie his front feet together. And then you pull a hind foot up and that old horse won't be able to get up. If you leave his hind feet untied, he'll get up. In calf roping they use the two hind feet and the front foot. A horse is just the other way.

A horse that's down, then you can put your hackamore on his head, or breaking halter to break him to lead, however you want to do it. Like my father was saying, if you needed to ride that horse that day, if that's the only horse you got and you've got so much work to do and you've got to get going, you've got to get with it. You can't be a-doing it a half hour today and a half hour tomorrow. You've got to get to using him.

That's the way you end up once in a while. I remember when all the gentle horses got out and all I had left was one I hadn't used yet. Well, you either walk to get those others or you ride. Now, we was taught to ride! Walking came second.

And Dad taught us right quick that the safest place is on top of that horse. If you'd ever had a horse that knew how to shake hands with you, biting or striking at you, then you'd begin to understand what that means. When you're getting your foot in the stirrup you can have an old horse reach out there and bite you in the rump or kick your foot out of the stirrup. Every horse has got a different personality. They all got these different tricks.

That's where the techniques start coming in—like these breaking hackamores. You get that snitched down there so's it's around the horn and get your elbow about right. Get things done without making a big issue and he learns, but you don't tease or hurt him. Just discipline him at the right time. Around here we say get a sarviceberry bush. That's a switch. If he does something you don't like, that's when you pop him on the nose. Or if he bites your foot in the stirrup, kick him in the nose. He might try to buck you off, but he won't bite your foot again. It's important how you keep things under control.

This is a catch rope and this round corral is used when you're starting a horse if you want to teach him to change his leads. A horse will lead out with one front foot. To make a real good reining horse you want him so that on cue he can change over and lead with his other foot. If he can't do that, he makes a rougher horse and it takes longer for him to turn. In training a neck-reined horse the ultimate goal is that he do this automatically when you touch his neck with your rein. That's the thing about a horse. If you're gonna ride him, you let him worry about where he's gonna put his feet to get you there. You just ask him to do it for you. And if he doesn't have the ability to do it for you, well, you trade him off and start out with something else. That's why in this horse business there's a horse for everybody but there isn't a horse for everything you want to get done. Like you've got good cutting horses, you've got good rope horses, you've got good pack horses, and you've got good bucking horses. Now, there's horses that are willing to buck but can't. They just kinda crow-hop around. But if they have the ability, they get so they kinda enjoy it. If he has the ability and you want him to be that way, you encourage it. Then you don't want to use him to plow a field or be in a pack string and go to the rodeo that weekend.

There was a fella by here talking about horses one time. I told him, You've gotta learn to read if you want to understand a horse. I says, Can't you read his eye? "Huh?" he said. "What do you mean?" He'd been telling me what a horseman he was. I said, Well, you'd better learn how to read that old pony's eye.

Sure. You can see fire come into a horse's eye if he gets mad at you. Then his eye gets red but he's still holding his temper and hasn't taken after you yet. Then you use a little more caution. You talk to him in a little different tone or say, "Hey, partner, stand there awhile while I go over here and think this over." I've been in them situations when I had a job to do. Once I had to pack to get going and got my horse mad. So I stopped to figure out how to calm him down and still get the job done and git on up the trail. That's reading those eyes. If you see a spark come in their eye, you know good and well they're enjoying what they're doing. You get around them rodeos and it's time for that old pony to go out that chute, you'll see a spark there.

173

Ross Filer

"I belong to the cattle ever after"

If you saw a certain old cowhand moving creakily up the main street of Twisp, Washington, population 756, his red wheelbarrow piled high with cornstalks, you might wonder about the man's ability to reach his destination. "I can't get on a horse anymore," he'd say if he noticed your interest in his gait. "I'm too blamed stiff. I'm 76 years old and my best days are gone. I don't know, by gum, but I'm getting stiffer every year."

The permanent stubble of beard beneath a battered wool cap, the scribbled note ("Lots of ambition but I hate to waste it on work") pinned to his grimy jacket, the labored speech of someone whose teeth are mostly a memory, the knee-high black rubber boots. . . a Dostoyevsky reader would think immediately of a village idiot. Most drivers would not look twice at the dotard behind the slowly moving pile of silky, fresh corn leaves.

Twisp does have its share of village idiots. And they can be found every Saturday night trying to pick fights in the Antlers Tavern. Ross Filer is not one of them, but neither is he understood by any but the local old-timers. Even they were amazed recently when Ross published a dictated Western novel, The Silver Bell Cattle Company, or The Way Things Should Be. *Ask him to repeat any of that colorful story and he can do so verbatim—like an ancient, illiterate bard.*

"Ross Filer is not really crazy," says a Twisp friend, "but he lives in a different space which today's people don't understand." After a long life raising and fattening beef Ross Filer simply loves cows. He accounts for it by saying that he is "a natural-born cattleman," but that isn't much of an explanation. He continues, "It's like the cow horses I've seen that wouldn't pull a plough, that were balkier than. . ." His voice trails off as he searches for a comparison. "Oh hell," he explains, "they'd just kick things all to pieces if you tried to hitch 'em up."

Someone gave him the cornstalks to take home to grind up for feed, a characteristic Ross Filer effort on behalf of the few cows he keeps out on the edge of town. A note permanently attached to the door of his disorderly, gear-strewn cabin states, "To Who This May Concern: The Cattle Come First. I Belong To The Cattle Ever After. Find Me Wherever You Can. Ross."

Ross Filer's story goes back to 1889 when his uncle homesteaded in the Methow and operated a stage run to the Columbia River, where there was a steamboat connection to the railhead downstream at Wenatchee. Ross's parents arrived in 1900 with a wagon and buggy, driving cattle ahead of them. Ross was born in 1903, and as the country developed he worked as a drover for various ranchers, including his father.

Feed your calves skim milk, waste the manure which could be enriching your fields, or mistreat your stock and you will join a cast of local evildoers in Ross's ongoing narrative. If a wealth of cattle lore can make for eloquence, Ross Filer is the undiscovered sage of the Methow.

T alk about Jiminy Christmas! One of the main things is getting rid of them blamed horns. If you buy a bunch of horny cattle, you want to cut their horns off 'cause they'll just hog the feed. They'll just knock the daylights out of the others. And the others will starve and be poor as a snake. We had a great big shorthorn cow one time with great big horns that curved around. She'd knock heifers right off their grain, butt 'em in the ribs. Then I swear, talk about Jiminy Christmas, I got so mad at her! Well anyway, we cut the horns off of that cow and her scabs was just getting healed up. But one day she forgot she was dehorned and she hit a cow right in the ribs. And whoa! All the snorting you ever heard. Jiminy Christmas!

The thing is, you got to put your heart in what you're doing. You can ask people around here and they'll tell you that my stock always looked good. I take care of 'em and I know when they're putting on fat.

About July we'd gather all the cattle and put 'em on North Creek on the high range. We'd camp there. North Creek comes down in a big wide canyon. It's steep. By gum, it's about that steep. Water just boils out of those hills. Water's everywhere. When you get up there the dew is so heavy you'd think it was frost. The grass and weeds the cattle like are about two feet high.

If they're broke to the range, they'll go up there themselves. The Forest Service had to have a drift fence to keep 'em out of there until the right time. But in the fall of the year you've gotta go get 'em. There's stragglers that rustle off so you can't find 'em all.

I always got my cattle out before hunting season, because the hunters would kill 'em. They'd just take and shoot at anything. Anything. Any, any little thing. They don't care. They don't care. They're where they don't belong. Oh, I'll tell you, it's the same all over the United States. Ellensburg's having the same trouble. Hunters!

Well anyway, on the high range you don't have to do a lot of work. Just scatter the salt. You don't have to fight 'em. Never fight 'em. Don't fight 'em any more than you have to. The more you can leave 'em alone the better off you are.

When I went up to take care of the cattle, the first thing I did was get my dinner. You have to find your water and build your campfire. Scrape away all burnable material and dig a hole about one foot wide and four feet long. Your fire is right down there in the hole. Then you put across there your camp irons, pieces of pipe. If you haven't got any camp irons, you can cut a little tree and make some. Of course, they won't let you do nothin' like that now, by gum. So don't you do that. Well, then you put your kettle on the camp irons. Get willow, birch, or alder, wood that don't

throw any sparks. Fir throws too much sparks. Pine don't throw very many. Have a bucket of water in case anything happens.

When you cook your breakfast or dinner make a very little fire. You don't want a big fire because it would be so doggone hot. Your bacon or whatever would burn up and the grease in your skillet would catch on fire.

I always made a big bunch of stew and a bunch of beans. Nothing tastes so good when you come in as to have a big plate of brown beans and some bread. Of course, making beans you want to put in plenty of water or you'll have a devil of a time. They'll stick to the kettle and you'll have to scrape 'em out. With stew, take meat and potatoes and onions, carrots, anything you want to put in there. Two tablespoons full of salt. I had the best of meat because we used to butcher these Black Angus cattle. You bet you life it was delicious!

And after you get your water and your fire you set up your canvas tent and get it ready. I never slept in the tent unless it was stormy. I'd sleep outside on boughs—but they won't let you do that anymore either. If I could find a hole in the ground, I'd always put my bed in there. I liked to hear the river roar and I liked to hear the chipmunks and I liked to hear the magpie and I liked to hear the hooter. Well, I've slept all over, on hillsides, up against logs, but I was young in those days.

After my father died in 1938, Mother and I held onto the cattle and raised hay. I did everything with horses. I never did own a tractor. I had a four-horse spring tooth. Even now if you gave me a field and some horses, I could do it right. But with a tractor I'd get ridges. We kept our cattle till 1945. By then the Forest Service made it hard on range cattle. Mother died in 1949.

Riding herd, driving those cattle, doing that was my pleasure. You got hot and you got cold and you worked hard, but that was my heaven.

Thong Nguyen

Refugee

◈

Thong Nguyen was born in 1938 in Hanoi in the French colony of Indochina. War, war, and more war has been the fate of that land since ancient times. It was Thong Nguyen's personal fate as well until April 25, 1975, when he found himself putting out to sea in an overcrowded boat with other refugees from the final siege of Saigon.

America has always been a country focused on the future, and for some it is as daunting a frontier as ever. The other men and women in this book recall an earlier frontier, but it is worth remembering, and Thong Nguyen reminds us, that we all move forward with the momentum of our refugee beginnings.

There is nothing reassuring about the future. All we have is our faith. Back at some point in each of our family histories we voted for the future with our feet. Thong Nguyen did too, and in the most dramatic of circumstances. He has since built a new family, two houses, the American dream.

Once on that boat there is no turning back. We Americans belong to the future.

179

We have had war in my country all the time. For a thousand years we had to fight with the Chinese. And eighty years with the French. And then the Americans were in South Vietnam fighting with the Communists. And right now the Communists keep fighting, fighting.

When your country is at war and you are eighteen or twenty-one years old you have no choice. You have to go in the army.

My last rank was Major but I was promoted to Lieutenant Colonel just before leaving. I think I was a good army commander because I won most of the time on the battlefield. That means you have to be smart—to know when, where, and why to fight with the enemy. Most of the time I won. I fought all over in a moving battalion of four to six hundred men, wherever the army needed support.

I was born in Hanoi, which I remember as a beautiful country. A lot of things are in my memory about what a good area for living it was. In Hanoi there were two lakes inside the city. Very beautiful. Seattle reminds me of Hanoi.

We had a big family there. My grandmother, my parents, and my younger and older brothers and sisters. Eleven children. I am the middle one, the fourth, in my family. All of us lived together except my oldest brother who was a student in France.

In 1954, about one year after Dien Bien Phu, when I was fourteen, we had to leave the north. The Communists gave a 24-hour deadline for the people who wanted to leave. And my parents decided that we'd go, that we could not stay. We took the last plane at the last minute. We couldn't take anything. I still remember that when we left Hanoi my parents only had very little money. But my father was a famous businessman in construction and he had some friends in Saigon who helped him to start over again in South Vietnam.

In 1954 you had a little bit of time to make a decision to stay or go. But in 1975 the situation in South Vietnam was very, very panicky. Terrible. Just terrible.

I was lucky to get out of my country. If I had stayed . . . When the Communists took over Saigon they put a lot of my friends, same promotion and rank, in a reeducation camp. They're still in there. Maybe some of them have been killed. I didn't make a decision to leave. I was just lucky. But that's the reason why I lost my family. At the very last minute I was fighting in Saigon with the enemy at one very important spot. And I tried to communicate with some officers higher than me, like a general, and no answer. So I thought they were gone. We were fighting but without support like ammunition or someone to come and help us. So I told the soldiers under my command, I said, We're fighting now over here by ourselves and we could be killed very soon because we've almost finished the ammunition. I told them, Well, you stay or go. But I have to go somewhere. I don't know where but I have to go somewhere.

There was one area on the river where my enemy hadn't come yet. I met a friend there who was the commander of the last army boat. And we went down the river. He took his family, too.

I lost my family, but you know, right now we can talk about why we acted like we did. But if you were me. . . the situation at the last minute was the very worst panic. You could not think what you wanted to do or where you wanted to go. Well, we went down the river and got on the Pacific Ocean and met about forty boats and big ships. And we transferred to a big American cargo boat. And they brought us to Guam.

The first day when I arrived in Seattle was very strange for me. Everything. People. Tradition. Customs. Weather. It was a big change for me. My eyes were just like big open. I looked around. Very strange.

I met my sponsor, Randy Urmston, because of my sister. She's working now at the World Bank in Washington, D.C. But then she was a student here at the University of Washington. She explained to the people at Saint Mark's Cathedral that she had a brother at Camp Pendleton and that she needed a sponsor for him. Then a young lawyer named Randy Urmston who had been an American army officer in my country volunteered to be a sponsor for me.

I came to Seattle July 2, two days before Independence Day. Summertime. I remember it was very funny. Why so funny? Because some American people at Camp Pendleton had told me that Seattle was very wet and cold. So when I came here I wore a lot of clothes like an Eskimo man. But when

I went out of the airplane the weather was hot. People were surprised at my big coat.

Because we Vietnamese cannot go back to our country we try to adjust to the new living over here. We have no choice.

It's hard to explain why someone is successful. Sometimes people are lucky. But if you want to be lucky, you have to prove something first. That means you have to try to work hard. If you don't, even if you have luck you cannot be successful.

Two weeks after I got here my sponsor Randy introduced me to everything in Seattle. And I went to his law office every day and met his friends and talked about the new life for me over here. And about English. But I told Randy that I did not want to burden him. I said I could do two things. At night I'd go to school, and in the daytime I could work. One of Randy's friends introduced me to someone at City Ice and Cold Storage who gave me a job. So in just two weeks I had found a job.

My company gets bigger every day. They just changed the name, but it's the same people, the same boss. Seapro—seafood processing.

In my country I was a high official. And I had a degree from the Vietnam Military Academy. The same program as West Point. I am not a dummy. I am smart. But when you start work somewhere. . . . Right now I understand—if you start work somewhere, you start at the bottom first. It was very awful for me the first week at work. I had to do labor work. I had not lifted the heavy things before because I was a commander. In my country I never touched things like that. But I had to do labor work here. My feelings. . . I was awful mad. You know, I worked and I cried, both. I didn't know why I had to do like that. If my country hadn't fallen to the Communists, maybe in the future I would have been a general.

But I tried to forget about the past and to think about the future and the present. And I tried to do as I could—labor work, everything. And after that I had some ideas. After work I talked to my foreman and supervisors and gave them some ideas about the work. The bosses were smart people, but nobody is perfect. They can't see everything. After work I talked to them and suggested how to use a machine to reduce hand labor. Because

I had some ideas for them they knew I was a smart guy. And after that they gave me a raise and I moved up.

When you work on an assembly line you have to go fast every day. If you don't, you back up everything and there's not enough money for the company. The fresh fish and the frozen fish are in the assembly line. Somebody grades them and somebody bags them and puts them in a box and after that they're run through the scale. At the scale you have to make even weight for each box. Different sizes like 50 or 100 or 200 pounds. Well, I have a feeling about what kind of fish weighs how much. If I look at a fish, I can judge how many pounds that fish has, so I can quickly make the even weight on the scale. So when I worked on the scale, we'd go fast every day. Every day we'd go better and better. My boss said, ''Thong is smart and does a very good job on the electric scale.'' So I was promoted to scale work.

When I got my job at City Ice, I worked hard at everything. I helped other people when I was finished with my own work. I think America needs some people like that who are not lazy at work. I think if you have money and you have a company, you need smart people and good workers. You don't need the lazy people. Every day I was working hard. I told my boss, I don't mind overtime and I can stay and help. I tried to finish the job and not leave everything like that for tomorrow. The fish would spoil.

My own idea is that our Vietnamese people were working hard in our country before we came here. When you start over again, if you want to have your own property, you have to work hard and save money. My Vietnamese friends here are successful, too, because they try to work hard every day. That's our national tradition.

Glossary

bannock: biscuit dough cooked in a frying pan.

barber chair: a stump which has split while being cut, leaving a piece of wood standing up.

beer: a fermented mash used to make moonshine.

bindle: a bundle carrying a wanderer's possessions.

blinds: the platform immediately behind a train engine's tender.

boondog: to drift down a river while fishing.

bow and arrow horse: a mustang or Indian pony.

brail: to hoist fish out of a fish trap with a net.

bull block: a large wide-throated pulley for collecting logs.

camp irons: homemade endirons used as a platform for campfire pots.

cant hook: a sturdy lever with a blunt end and a movable hook used in logging.

cat face: a tree with burnt-in black spots.

cayuse: a mustang or Indian pony.

chicken moat: a chickenpen built to enclose a garden, enabling the chickens to eat invading grasshoppers.

clearcut: to remove all the trees in a given area.

cuttyhunk line: a braided cotton fishing line made in Japan.

dally: to wind the rope around the saddle horn before roping an animal.

dog: a metal hook for holding a log.

fall: to cut down trees.

fish trap: a pilings and net device for catching fish.

footburner plough: a simple plough guided by a person on foot and pulled by horses.

four-horse spring tooth: a horse-pulled harrow with flexible, curved teeth.

gill netter: a fishing boat equipped with a vertically suspended mesh net that entraps the heads of fish.

grubhoe: a heavy hoe.

grubstake: a loan or gift to finance a prospecting trip or other enterprise.

hackamore: a halter used especially for breaking horses.

hardy: a blacksmith's chisel with a square shank that fits into a hole in the anvil.

hooter: the male grouse.

jackpot: a large logjam on a stream.

jammer: a mechanical hoist for loading logs.

kleutchman: Chinook jargon for woman.

latigo: a strap for tightening and fastening a saddle cinch.

mackinaw: a heavy wool coat.

Malone pants: heavy wool pants.

mercantile: general store.

Molly Hogan: a knot in a logger's steel cable.

peavey: a lever similar to the cant hook except for its sharp spike on the end.

placer mining: mining by washing sand and gravel for minerals.

pike pole: used by river pigs for handling floating logs.

pulaski: a single-bit axe with an adze-shaped grubhoe; named for its inventor, Edward Pulaski.

purse seine: a weighted net which closes on the bottom, entrapping a school of fish.

revenooer: a revenue officer, especially one who searched for illegal liquor during Prohibition.

river pig: a lumberjack who controls the logs as they float downriver to the sawmill.

rod: the metal framework beneath a railway car.

sack: to patrol a stream for stray logs at the end of a log drive.

saltchuck: salt water.

sarviceberry: juneberry or serviceberry (genus *Amelanchier*).

schoolmarm: a tree with a fork.

scow: a large, flat-bottomed transport boat that uses a large net which hangs vertically under water (see purse seine).

set choker: to attach a noose-like wire rope to a log so that it can be skidded.

shoty: tool for cutting hot steel

skag: cormorant

skid: to drag a log from its stump; a skidder is a log-moving tractor.

skinner: an animal driver.

slue: to turn or twist something around.

sluice box: a box for washing minerals out of sand and gravel (see placer mining).

snitch: to knot; a snitch is a woven knot.

soak: to pawn something.

sougan: a logger's cotton-filled comforter.

spiller: a fish trap's business end, from which trapped fish are brailed onto a scow.

sporting woman: a prostitute.

steam donkey: a movable steam engine used for skidding logs by cable.

strawberry: fish bait made of salmon eggs in a tiny cheesecloth bag.

swamp: to cut limbs off felled trees in preparation for skidding.

Swedish fiddle: two-man ''misery whip'' saw for felling large trees.

tamarack: the larch (genus *Larix*).

thrasher: a migrant worker who threshes grain.

timber cruiser: a forester who estimates types and quantities of trees in a given area.

tinhorn: a boastful gambler with little money.

tote road: a lumber camp's supply road.

Trapper Nelson: a Yukon pack frame originally made from a washboard.

turkey bell: a small bell used by steelhead fishermen as an alarm when a fish strikes.

wanigan: the company store in a logging camp.